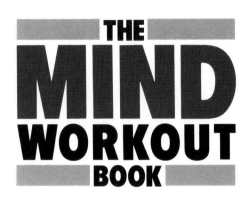

THE MIND WORKOUT BOOK

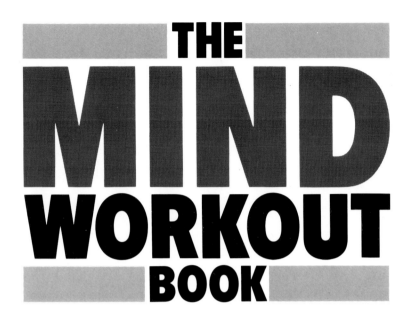

Dr Vernon Coleman

Viscount

Editor Carolyn Pyrah
Art Editor Sandra Horth
Copy Editor Linda Doeser
Design Malcolm Smythe
Illustration Anni Axworthy (*cartoons*);
Jim Robins (*21st century man*)
Artwork Keith Shannon, Hayward Art
Group and Stefan Chabluk
Studio Del & Co.
Production Controller Claire Kane
Picture Research Julia Pashley

This edition published in 1989 by
Viscount Books, an imprint of
The Hamlyn Publishing Group Limited
a division of the
Octopus Publishing Group
Michelin House
81 Fulham Road
London SW3 6RB

ISBN 0-600-566-471

Produced by Mandarin Offset
Printed in Hong Kong

The Publishers wish to thank the
following photographers and
organizations for their kind permission
to reproduce the photographs in this
book:
Allsport/Olitennent 6; Cannon 25;
Powell 122; Barry Ambrose 24;
Bridgeman Art Library/The Prado,
Madrid 64; © ADAGP, Paris, DACS,
London 1989 88; Britain On View
96t&c, 97cr; Camera Press Ltd 21, 62,
120; Susan Griggs/Horst Munzig 108;
The Image Bank 140; Robert Harding
Picture Library 74, 99c; Kobal
Collection 15c, 49, 102; Andrew
Lawson 96b; Natural History
Photographic Agency 94r, 95tl, tr&b;
Retna Pictures Ltd 15r, 76; Rex
Features Ltd 15tl; Science Photo
Library 28; Malcolm Smythe 72, 112;
Spectrum Colour Library 100t; Tony
Stone Associates 97b, 99b; Transworld
Features 13, 157; Venice-Simplon-
Orient Express Ltd 98t&c; Elizabeth
Whiting & Associates Ltd 97cl, Zefa
Picture Library 91, 92, 93, 94t, l&b, 97t,
98b, 99t, 100.

The following photographs were
specially taken for the Octopus
Publishing Group Picture Library: John
Freeman 95c; Melvin Grey 95tl; Sandra
Lousada 150.

Contents

Introduction

The Power
of Your Mind

When training his crew to win The America's Cup, yachtsman Dennis Connor recognized the importance of psychological preparation. 'I tried to get the boys to imagine how good it would feel to execute the perfect cast off or the perfect jibe. I asked them to imagine what it would be like to perform to complete perfection. I told them to capture the image of that perfection in their mind's eye ... If you can visualize something, you can actualize it.' (See page 25).

Let me start by telling you a story – a true story about a friend of mine called Tom. For several weeks he had a number of persistent and uncomfortable chest symptoms. He had a cough that would not go away and he had some difficulty in getting his breath. The symptoms were quite serious. His doctor tried all the usual drugs, but none of them seemed to work. Although he still managed to get to work, Tom found his symptoms annoying, troublesome and tiring.

Eventually, his family doctor referred him to a specialist at a nearby hospital. The consultant was puzzled but suggested that Tom should spend a few days in hospital so that some tests could be done. After a week, he was sent home. He was no better and no worse, but he had been assured that someone from the hospital would telephone the results of his tests as soon as possible. It was several days before someone rang – and then the news was devastating. The hospital spokesman explained to Tom's wife that the tests had shown a fast-growing cancer. The consultant, it was reported, predicted a rapid decline and death within a month or two.

Within two days Tom had started to deteriorate. The consultant's predictions were coming true. For the first time since the illness began, Tom could not get out of bed. Work became impossible and he felt so weak that he could not eat properly. He began to lose weight and he soon needed constant nursing. Relatives came from all over the country to await the predicted outcome. The house remained quiet, the curtains were drawn and people shuffled around quietly and timidly – talking in whispers.

Then came the second telephone call from the hospital. An apologetic voice told Tom's wife that a mistake had been made. He did not have cancer at all. There had been a mix-up. He had an infection that could be treated with special drugs. Within 24 hours Tom was out of bed and back at work. He could walk and eat again. He still had the chest symptoms, but he was no longer dying.

I have started with this brief but remarkable anecdote because it shows just how powerful the human mind can be. We tend to think of voodoo as a joke. We think it is bizarre that there are people living in

Africa or the West Indies who can be so terrified by a threat from a witch-doctor that they will go home and quietly die. Yet the only difference is that our witch-doctors wear white coats and stethoscopes instead of grass skirts and hideous masks. The plain truth is that there is nothing in this world which has such a far-reaching effect on your health as your mind. The way you respond to stress, pressure and worry will determine the condition of your heart, circulatory system, stomach, respiratory system and every other organ and tissue in your body. It is your state of mind which determines what diseases you will develop and how long you will live.

When Tom was told he was going to die, then he started to die. Obediently and politely his mind started to kill his body – fulfilling the prediction made by the doctors. He believed that the doctors knew best and his imagination did the rest. When he was told that there had been a mistake and that he was not going to die, he made an apparently miraculous recovery.

My friend Tom is by no means the only individual who has begun to die (or even has died) because of the power of the mind and the strength of the imagination. The writer T.H. White, author of *The Sword in The Stone* and *The Goshawk*, tells a story about an old man who lay on his deathbed for days and days, only just alive but apparently unable to drift into the peaceful arms of death. Eventually, his relatives remembered that he had always worn a good luck charm around his neck. He had never removed it throughout his life and had always believed that it gave him superhuman powers and provided him with some protection against death. When one of the relatives plucked up the courage to cut the chain and gently remove the charm from around the old man's neck he died quite quickly and peacefully.

The power of the human mind is truly extraordinary. Your mind can decide when you die and how you die. You may think I am exaggerating. You may even think I am talking total nonsense – and I certainly would not blame you for your scepticism. For years, the experts have told us that the only way to stay healthy is to eat nothing but good, wholesome food, to exercise regularly, to drive carefully and to drink in moderation. We are encouraged to visit the doctor whenever any signs or symptoms of illness develop. The medical profession has put a lot of effort – and a lot of our money – into the development of ever more sophisticated machinery designed to diagnose and treat disease at an early stage. There have been transplant operations, laser surgery, computer-managed diagnostic devices and test tube babies. It is difficult to switch on the television or to open a newspaper without finding yet more evidence showing that high-technology medicine has become an essential and accepted part of twentieth-century life.

But if you stop and consider for a minute, you will, I think, have to agree with me that things really have not gone as expected. Despite the fact that millions of people now avoid animal fats, food additives and cancer-inducing products such as tobacco, the incidence of illness continues to remain high. Indeed, there is now much evidence available to show that, instead of getting healthier, we are getting more sick.

There are many anomalies and mysteries too. Why does one man who smokes 60 cigarettes a day live to be 100, having never had a cough in his life, yet another, who has never smoked, dies at the age of 40 from lung cancer? Why does one man who eats a large, fatty breakfast enjoy perfect good health in his nineties, while another, who has avoided fatty foods like the plague, suddenly drops dead of a heart attack at the age of 35? Why does the woman who smokes too much, drinks too much and eats all the wrong things radiate good health? How can she burn the candle at both ends without ever getting her fingers burnt? Why does the young woman, who sticks to a vegetarian diet, only drinks bottled spring water, jogs twice a day for 40 minutes at a time and spends two hours a week in the gym, end up complaining of a thousand aches and pains? Why does the woman who spends her evenings at wild parties look ten years younger than she is, while the woman who lives on lentils and goes to bed at nine o'clock each evening looks ten years older than her real age?

In addition, why is it that, despite the fact that we are spending ever-increasing amounts of money on hospitals, screening clinics and wonderful new equipment, the evidence suggests that doctors are probably doing more damage – and causing more illness – than at any other time in history?

At the start of the twentieth century, the future looked bright. The drugs industry was just developing and surgical skills were being honed to new, high standards. Anyone alive at the start of this century would have felt confident that the medical profession would bloom and that, in future, people would lead longer and healthier lives. But that has not happened. Within the last 20 years, more money has been spent on health care and medical research than had been spent in the whole of the rest of our history on earth, but we have very little to show for it. Medicine has sunk into a slough and there has been almost no improvement in either the quality or quantity of life enjoyed in the developed countries of the world. The World Health Organization's figures suggest that in some developed countries there has, in recent years, been a decrease in life expectancy and an increase in the mortality rate among young people.

edicine has become full of confusions and paradoxes. During the last quarter of a century we have developed remarkably sophisticated machinery for our hospitals, and yet cancers, immune disorders and allergy problems become commoner day by day. We now have specialist coronary care units for heart attack victims, specialist ambulances and more heart specialists than ever before, and yet more people than ever are dying of heart disease. More and more people live in air-conditioned, centrally heated buildings, and yet infections kill millions.

There is probably no single, simple explanation for this disastrous state of affairs. In part, it is due to the fact that the medical profession has spent the last century creating a system of health care designed to suit its own needs rather than the needs of its patients. In part, the problem is due to the fact that doctors have taken too much control for themselves. Overcome with enthusiasm for the marvels of science, they have ignored the healing powers of the individual body. For the first time in history, we have a medical profession with the power to interfere with nature. Yet, for the first time in history, we have a medical profession which has chosen to ignore the phenomenon of natural healing. Doctors have become instilled with a sense of power and have taken too much responsibility and, out of a mixture of respect, admiration and fear, patients have let them take that responsibility.

The main reason why things have gone wrong is, I believe, that the modern doctor regards the human body as a machine. Today's doctor is trained to believe that, when symptoms develop or when the system is not functioning effectively, all you have to do is take the machine apart, examine the bits and pieces and fiddle with those parts which seem to be malfunctioning. It must be said that this simple, mechanistic approach has served science well for several centuries. For hundreds of years the basic aim of most medical treatments has been to suppress any signs or symptoms of illness as quickly and as efficiently as possible.

On the basis of this simple philosophy, health care has become one of the biggest industries in the world. Today, millions of people earn a good living by selling medical advice, therapeutic pills and promising potions. Orthodox practitioners and alternative health-care professionals alike compete to interfere, to intervene with nature, to offer magical solutions. We, of course, have welcomed their promises. We desperately want to believe in miracle medicine. We want to believe in wonder drugs and high-technology cures. We want to believe in them because these solutions are easier and more comfortable than changing our own life-styles. We want to believe in the philosophy of interventionism because, if it is true that the body is a machine, then we can conquer all illness by investing in high-technology medicine. We want to believe because, if it is true that the body is a machine, then we do not have to worry too much; we are free to hand over our health to the professionals. However, there is now a growing amount of irrefutable evidence that those traditional medical experts, the ones who believed that the body functions simply, like a machine, got it wrong.

The traditional healing approach is to treat the patient as a background, the illness as an enemy and the treatment as a weapon with which to fight the illness. Today, this interventionist approach is so strong that many patients will hesitate to deal even with mild symptoms without first asking for professional advice. But in recent years we have acquired considerable evidence to show that this is not always the best approach. The human body is, it seems, equipped with an enormous range of subtle and sophisticated feedback mechanisms. Some of these exist to help you fight off disease. Many are given the job of regulating what you eat and drink so that, if you listen to them, your body will be provided with the ingredients it really needs to stay healthy. Together these mechanisms mean that your body is well equipped to look after itself when threatened with disease and infection. There are internal mechanisms designed to enable you to avoid danger, deal with minor damage, cope with pain, improve your eyesight, keep out the cold, stay slim for ever, improve the shape of your body, deal with anxiety and even fight cancer. The body's defence mechanisms and self-healing mechanisms are so effective that, if you learn how to take advantage of them, then, in at least 90 per cent of all illnesses, you will get better without any form of medical treatment whatsoever.

Of course, you take many of your body's skills for granted, but even the responses which seem relatively straightforward are not necessarily as simple as you might imagine them to be. If you cut yourself, you expect the blood to clot and the wound to heal. It does not seem like anything special or particularly complicated. In practice, however, the blood clotting mechanism that you take for granted is part of a defence system they would have been proud to match at NASA.

network of fail-safe mechanisms ensures that the system is not triggered accidentally into action when there is no leak. More safety checks ensure that the clotting does not begin to operate until enough blood has flown through the injury site to wash away any dirt. Once the clot has formed and the loss of blood has been stopped, the damaged cells will release chemicals into the tissues. These chemicals are designed to make the local blood vessels expand. This in turn will ensure that extra quantities of blood flow into the injury site, making the area red, swollen and hot. The heat will help damage any infective organisms and the swelling will ensure that the injured part is not used too much. By immobilizing the area, the pain and the stiffness will act as a natural splint. White blood cells brought to the injury site will help by swallowing up any more debris or bacteria. These scavenging cells, bloated with rubbish, will be discharged from the body as pus, once they have done their job. Only after the debris has been cleared and the threat of infection removed, will the injury begin to heal. The scar tissue that forms will be stronger than the original skin.

All this assumes that the injury is a fairly small one and that the clotting mechanism can deal with the potential blood loss effectively. However, even if there is an appreciable blood loss, your body still has a number of other mechanisms designed to help you stay alive. Arteries supplying the injured area will constrict and so limit further blood losses. Peripheral blood vessels supplying the skin will shut down to ensure that the supply of blood to the more essential organs is preserved. The kidneys will cut off the production of urine so that fluid levels within the body are kept as high as possible. Fluids will be withdrawn from your tissues to dilate and increase the volume of the blood which remains. The red cell-producing sites within your body will step up production in order to replace the cells which have been lost. Finally, as an added refinement which any engineer would consider a touch of pure genius, the loss of blood will trigger off a thirst intended to ensure that the missing fluids are replaced as quickly as possible.

I have described the blood clotting mechanism at some length because it is one of the simplest and best known of all the body's defence mechanisms. There are many more.

If you go out for the evening and drink several pints of fluid, your kidneys will get rid of the excess. On the other hand, if you spend a hot day hiking and you drink very little, your kidneys will reduce your fluid output. While they are regulating fluid flow, your kidneys will also ensure that the salts, electrolytes and other essential chemicals in your body are kept balanced. If you eat too much table salt, for example, your kidneys will ensure that the excess is excreted and if you eat too many salted peanuts in a bar, your body will increase your natural thirst so that you will drink and hence be able to cope with the extra salt.

There are mechanisms designed to keep your internal temperature stable. Sitting in the sun makes your skin go pink because more fluid flows through the surface vessels of your body. This increase in superficial blood flow will enable your body to get rid of heat simply because the blood will lose heat to the surrounding air. You will sweat, too, as your body cunningly uses the fact that, when water evaporates, heat is lost. Incidentally, as the sweat pours out, so the amount of saliva you produce will fall, making your mouth dry. You will get thirsty and drink more fluids to replace the fluid your body is losing.

Should a speck of dust find its way into one of your eyes, tears will flood out in an attempt to wash the irritant away. The tears contain a special bactericidal substance designed to kill off any infection. Your eyelids will temporarily go into spasm to protect your eyes from further damage.

When you have a fever, the rise in tissue temperature is probably a result of your body's trying to help you cope more effectively with any infection that may be present. The temperature rise improves the capacity of the body's defence mechanisms, while at the same time threatening the existence of the invading organisms. It seems, too, that there is sense in the old theory that it is better to starve a fever than to force food down an unwilling patient's throat. Whereas the human body can survive without fresh food, living on its stored supplies, the bacteria which cause infection need fresh food if they are to live and breed.

Once you start looking at the mechanisms which exist inside the body, the powers revealed are so extensive and so amazing that it is difficult to know where to stop. Research has shown that the brain contains a natural tranquillizer designed to help you cope with anxiety, that pain thresholds and pain tolerance levels increase quite naturally during the final days of pregnancy, that breast milk contains a substance designed to tell a baby when he or she has had enough to eat and that during the years when a woman is fertile, the walls of her vagina produce a special chemical designed to reduce the risk of any local infection developing. If you do a lot of kneeling on hard surfaces, your knee caps will acquire a soft, squashy, protective swelling. If you eat something infected, you will vomit. If you get something stuck in your windpipe, you will cough it up. If you spend a lot of time in the sun, special pigmented cells will migrate to the surface of your skin to provide you with a layer of protection against its rays.

The evidence which shows the extent of the human body's healing powers is impressive enough, but this is only the beginning. There is now increasing evidence to show that our health is influenced not just by what we eat or how much exercise we take, and not just by our own bodies' internal protective mechanisms, but by our attitudes, our expectations, our hopes, our moods, our personalities and our temperaments. Our health is not just influenced by physical forces but by mental forces too – and these mental forces are far more powerful and have a far greater effect on our health than any other factor.

Your body has natural ways of preserving its equilibrium. An example of this is when, in the heat of the sun, your temperature is kept at a safe level through perspiration: mechanisms increase the amount of fluid coursing through the surface vessels, cooling the blood (and making your skin pink), while beads of sweat lose heat on the body as they evaporate.

A few years ago the majority of medical scientists would have laughed at the idea of there being any real link between problems in the mind and problems affecting the body. Today, I very much doubt if there is a doctor or reputable medical scientist anywhere in the world who does not accept that stress, fear, worry, apprehension, anger and anxiety can all cause genuine physical responses and real diseases. The figures vary from report to report but, at a conservative estimate, at least three quarters of all the problems seen by doctors are illnesses which originate either completely or partly in the mind. I believe that between 90 and 95 per cent of all illnesses can be blamed totally or partially on psychological forces. Our minds are killing us.

In the last few years many papers have been published showing how damaging stress can be produced. A report published recently showed that the type of depression which often follows a bereavement can affect the body's internal defence mechanisms so violently that small, cancerous tumours which might otherwise have been suppressed by the body's own defences can survive, grow and eventually kill the patient. Another report demonstrated that the immune system of a recently bereaved individual shows a marked reduction in efficiency: sadness changes the body's ability to cope with disease. A third study has shown that, within eight weeks of the death of a close relative, our bodies become so badly damaged by bereavement that they are exceptionally vulnerable to cancers and infections of all kinds. A fourth study reveals that the death rate among widowed individuals is 12 times the rate among non-bereaved individuals.

Of course, many people could have told you all this years ago, without scientific papers to prove the points. It has been widely understood for centuries that when one partner dies the other, previously apparently fit and healthy, will often die too. The young woman who pines away and dies after her soldier lover is killed at war is not just a figment of the imagination. The difference is that there is now evidence available to prove these suspicions. If you are under pressure at home or your love life is too hectic, your chances of having a heart attack are six times greater than normal. The same is true if you have money worries or problems involving close friends. If you are socially 'upwardly mobile' (ambitious, earning more money, looking for better jobs, moving to a bigger house and so on), that can increase your chances of having a heart attack three or four times.

Each month something like 6,000 medical journals are published around the world. A growing number of them are carrying reports of new evidence which illustrates the existence and importance of the link between mental pressure and physical and mental disease. As long ago as 1946, a research project, started in America and involving 1,500 medical students, was designed to investigate the relationship between attitudes and illness. The research programme lasted for 17 years and suggested that the way an individual responds to pressure has a powerful effect on the types of illness his or her body develops.

In 1948, Dr Barbara Betz, a psychiatrist, started a similar research project which lasted for 30 years. She studied 45 students and classified them as Alphas (steady, cautious and self-reliant), Betas (easy going, cheerful and spontaneous) or Gammas (moody, quick to anger and either

over- or under-demanding). Thirty years later, when she analysed her data, she found that 25 per cent of the students classified as Alphas had developed severe mental or physical illness, while 26.7 per cent of the students classified as Betas had developed serious illness. The most staggering discovery, however, was the fact that 77.3 per cent of the Gammas had developed severe mental or physical illness.

recent conference in Canada was nearly unanimous in agreeing that a patient's attitude towards life directly affects both his physical and mental health. The link between the mind and the body can produce a constricting, destructive circle of endless distress. Even worrying about illness can produce illness.

The relationship between the mind and the body is so powerful that even when a disease or an injury has been caused by some entirely external force, the attitude of the patient can have a powerful effect on the speed with which the damaged parts of the body recover. If you fall down while skiing and you break your leg, the rate at which the broken bones will mend depends upon your attitudes, hopes, fears and aspirations. If you decide that you are going to be crippled for months, you probably will be. If you decide that you are going to be crippled for life, the chances are that you will be.

A doctor I know, who works as a medical officer for a football team, told me not long ago about two players who had suffered very similar injuries. The first player, Michael, was bitter and resentful. He was angry because the opponent who had fouled him had not been booked by the referee or punished by his team. He was worried about his place in the team because he was only too well aware that a younger player, who had come up from the reserves to substitute for him, was taking advantage of the opportunity to impress the team manager. The second player, Tony, was much calmer and more relaxed, even though his circumstances were very similar. He spent hardly any time brooding, but concentrated on getting back to full match fitness.

Television series and films offer clear-cut fictional examples of different personality types. John-boy Walton (left) typifies the Alpha character, which is reliable and steady. Beta types are easy going and spontaneous, as personified by Crocodile Dundee (centre), while Alexis of *Dynasty* (right) is the epitome of the over-demanding prima donna.

As you have undoubtedly guessed by now, Tony was back in the first team within a couple of months. Michael, the player who had spent his time worrying, was still hobbling around leaning on a walking stick.

Once it became clear that the mind has great power over the body, scientists started to look for ways to explain this phenomenon. The first major discovery was that the mind exerts much of its most potent power through the medium of the imagination. The simple and astonishing truth is that our bodies are often affected, not by what has happened or is about to happen, but by what we think has happened and what we believe is likely to happen. If you believe that you are going to be fired from your job, your body will respond in the same dramatic way that it would if you really were fired from your job. If you really, truly and honestly believe that you are pregnant, then your periods will stop, your breasts will swell and you will put on weight.

I first became aware of the power of the imagination when I read a report about something that had happened when the film *Lawrence of Arabia* was first shown in the cinema. It contained a number of long desert scenes in which Peter O'Toole, the star of the movie, was wandering around on a camel, parched and weary. Almost everywhere the film was shown, cinema managers noticed the same thing: the sales of cold drinks and ice creams rocketed. The only possible conclusion was that the scorching desert scenes had made the patrons feel uncomfortably hot and their bodies had responded to what they were seeing.

You can test this influence for yourself next time you watch a film on television or rent a video. If the film you are watching contains lots of shots of explorers in the Arctic or Antarctic huddled together in igloos, with icicles on their beards and their sleeping bags frozen solid, you will probably notice that the people who are watching with you are shivering, complaining about the cold and reaching to switch up the heating. If the film is frightening, with lots of shots of dark passageways and creepy murderers, conversely the people with you will be biting their fingernails, covering their eyes with their hands, imagining noises in the house and rushing outside during the advertisements to check that the back door is firmly locked and bolted.

Indeed, film directors deliberately use our imaginations to help them create better scenes. In traditional cowboy films, the good guys wore white and the bad guys wore black because, from experience, that is what we have come to expect. Once we see a man in white, our imagination does the rest. Red cars are usually driven by aggressive people, red clothes are worn by sexy women and so on.

If your imagination is reasonably good, you can, of course, obtain exactly the same sort of real physical response simply by reading a well-written book. If the story is sad, the tears will start to pour down your cheeks. If it is dramatic and you are worried about the safety of the hero, your heart will beat faster. If it is frightening, the hairs on the back of your neck will stand up. In each case, your body is responding not to reality (you may be reading your book while lying comfortably in bed or in the bath), but to your imagination.

Hypnotism and hypnotherapy are often linked with darkened rooms with drawn curtains, soft voices, swinging fob watches and long leather

*P*ersonality *P*rism

Your favourite colours – those you usually choose to wear – give away a lot about your personality. The clothes you choose for particular occasions tell a lot about your mood at the time.

RED
Impulsive · Aggressive · Creative · Intense · Sensual · Sexual · Energetic · Forceful

ORANGE
Confused · Uncertain · Looking for Change and Confrontation

YELLOW
Wise · Logical · Knowledgeable · Unemotional · Cool · Detached

GREEN
Accurate · Precise · Obsessive · Consistent · Proud · Envious · Peaceful

BLUE
Placid · Calm · Tranquil · Self-assured · Relaxed · Balanced · Loyal

INDIGO
Mysterious · Spiritual · Ritualistic · Philosophical

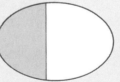

VIOLET
Insecure · Immature · Irresponsible

couches. Frequently associated with quacks, charlatans, cheap diplomas and dishonest practitioners anxious to obtain financial or sexual favours from their patients, hypnotherapy is, in fact, a genuine way of using the power of the imagination.

The first evidence that hypnotherapy could have useful effects was produced in 1847, when James Esdale performed 300 major surgical operations in India using no anaesthetic other than hypnosis. Since then, scores of other researchers have shown that by hypnotizing patients and putting them into an altered state of consciousness, it is possible to combat many different kinds of pain and discomfort. These days, numerous women have babies under hypnosis and many operations are performed with no other anaesthetic. You do not, however, have to see a hypotherapist in order to benefit from the power of hypnotherapy. You can easily hypnotize yourself – simply by harnessing the power of your imagination. It is your imagination that is the key which will unlock this powerful force.

Scientists have shown that the power of the imagination is so overwhelming that apparently involuntary reflexes can be controlled by thought processes. For example, in one experiment volunteers were able to produce enzymes which their bodies did not need. Normally, if human beings eat meals that contain a good deal of fat, their bodies produce special enzymes to break it down and turn it into products which can be readily transported in the blood. These enzymes are produced without any thought and their production is controlled by a series of reflexes. However, under experimental conditions, it was shown that if volunteers were told that they had eaten fat when they had not, their bodies responded not to the reality, but to the imagined truth. The fat-dissolving enzymes were produced.

here is even a good deal of evidence to show that when doctors treat their patients, the expectations of the patient will have a powerful influence on the effectiveness of the treatment. One of the first doctors to report this unusual power was Dr Henry Beecher. When working as an American army medical officer during World War II, Beecher ran out of morphine while treating injured soldiers. Rather than admit to the soldiers (many of whom were suffering terrible injuries) that he had nothing to give them, he found some vials of plain water and injected those. To his astonishment, the water proved to be as powerful a painkiller as the missing morphine.

After the war, Beecher conducted many experiments to investigate the power of the imagination and the influence it could have on the efficacy of medical treatment. He also reported other experiments. One of the most remarkable involved patients suffering from angina – heart pain. The patients were told that they were going to have arterial by-pass surgery to cure their pain. They were, however, simply taken into the operating theatre, cut open and then sewn up again. Nothing else was done. Remarkably, these patients, who *expected* to feel better afterwards, did just as well as the patients who had had real by-pass surgery.

When I was a family doctor, I saw plenty of clinical evidence that the body's immune system can be influenced by the imagination. For example, I remember one patient, called Malcolm, who was a constant sufferer from hay fever, an allergy disorder that depends, to a large extent, upon the body's immune defence systems getting out of control. For some reason, the body recognizes pollen as an enemy and prepares its own defences. The idea is to get rid of the pollen as quickly as possible and the symptoms of hay fever are designed to do just that. Tears are produced to wash it away from the eyes and sneezes are started to empty the nose. It is an efficient, but potentially very annoying, over-reaction.

Malcolm was allergic to a huge number of different plants, but flowers were his main problem. Whenever he got near flowers of any kind he would sneeze endlessly, his eyes would run and he would look very uncomfortable. I proved that Malcolm's symptoms were not entirely physical when he came to see me one day and started sneezing as soon as he approached a vase of flowers left by another patient. He was quite indignant that I should have allowed anyone to leave flowers in the room when I knew that he was coming. What he did not know, however, was that the flowers were made of silk. They were completely artificial – Malcolm's imagination had done the rest.

Since there is now considerable evidence to suggest that the human body's immune system may well be linked to the development of many of the most destructive diseases of the twentieth century – including rheumatoid arthritis and some forms of cancer – the significance of the link between the imagination and the body's immune responses cannot be overestimated. Once you start looking for links between the imagination and the body, it is not difficult to find many more examples.

It is remarkably easy to prove to yourself the power of the imagination. For example, put a wooden plank on the floor and walk along it. You will almost certainly find it ridiculously easy. Now, tell yourself that the plank is suspended 500 feet up in the air and that if you fall, you will be dashed to death on rocks below. Try to see the huge chasm beneath you. Then try walking along the plank. The piece of wood will not have changed in width and it will still be resting on the floor, but you will find walking along it a much more difficult task.

I have wandered rather a long way from Tom, the friend whose story I described at the start of this introduction, but I hope that you will already agree with me that the power of the mind over the body is far too important to ignore.

n the past, doctors and health experts have always emphasized the benefits of maintaining a healthy body – exercising regularly and eating sensibly. Undoubtedly this can and does help you keep fit, but today there is ample evidence to show that it is at least as important to maintain a healthy mind. Your mind can make you ill – and, if you know how to use it, your mind can make you well again!

In 1964, Norman Cousins, then editor of *Saturday Review*, was taken ill with what his doctors diagnosed as ankylosing spondylitis – a degenerative disease of the spine. He was told by his medical advisers that the disease would cripple him permanently and would gradually paralyze his body. He was given the awful choice of having his body frozen in a lying down position or in a sitting upright position.

Cousins was not prepared to take these gloomy predictions lying down – or sitting up, for that matter. He remembered reading that stress and anxiety could have an adverse effect on the human body and could cause many types of severe illness. He assumed that if stress could have a damaging effect on the human body, the reverse should also be true – positive emotions, such as laughter, happiness, love and faith, should be able to help combat disease and promote good health. Inspired by his new theory and determined not to abandon himself to his fate, Cousins discharged himself from hospital (he later pointed out that a hospital is the last place on earth that someone who is sick should be taken) and checked into a hotel across the street. There, he claimed, the service was better, the cost was less and the comfort was greater. He then proceeded to surround himself with films and books that he knew would cheer him up. He acquired a projector and a collection of Marx Brothers films and he stocked up his library with books by authors such as P.G. Wodehouse, James Thurber and S.J. Perelman.

To his delight, Norman Cousins found that ten minutes of genuine amusement would give him hours of pain-free sleep. It was not until ten years later, in the mid-1970s, that scientists discovered that the brain can produce special proteins, called endorphins, which are the body's naturally produced equivalent of morphine. It was eventually shown that laughing and feeling relaxed and happy triggers the production of these endorphins. At the time, Cousins did not know what was happening – he only knew that his theory was correct. Laughing *did* make him feel better.

But laughing was not only making Cousins *feel* better. It was also having a genuine and measurable effect on the severity of his illness. Blood tests done in the hospital laboratory across the street from the hotel showed that, after he had watched a good film or read an enjoyable book, the disease that had threatened his life began to abate. To the astonishment of the doctors, it was shown that laughing produced a laboratory-measurable improvement in the ankylosing spondylitis.

Norman Cousins was undoubtedly one of the first to combat a serious illness in such a dramatic way. But during the last few years, there have been many other examples of men and women proving that the human mind has awe-inspiring power over the human body.

When I was a young family doctor, I looked after a young woman, called Pam, who had cancer of the bowel and who should have died within a matter of weeks, according to the hospital specialists who were involved in her care. She did not die and she would not even stay in hospital. She was not married, but she had three small children and she insisted on going home to look after them. The laboratory tests that the hospital doctors organized showed that she ought to have been dead, but she was not. She got thinner and thinner and began to look more and more like a skeleton, but still she did not die.

Everyone involved in her care found it baffling. It was difficult to understand just what was keeping her alive. It certainly was not anything that anyone had prescribed for her. The drugs that the hospital consultants had prescribed had made her feel sick and she had steadfastly refused to take them. Eventually, Pam got so weak and frail that she agreed to go into the hospital for a short rest. Her one condition was that her three children should be looked after by the same family and should not be split up. That was, it suddenly seemed to me, the key to everything. She would not consider going into hospital if it meant that her children had to be separated.

Finding a home for the children was not easy. The social workers I approached wanted to split up the family and put the children into separate foster homes. Homes that could cope with three new children all at the same time were not available. Just as I was about to despair of ever finding an answer, a chance conversation led to a foster family where the three children could stay together.

So Pam went into hospital and her children went to stay with temporary foster parents. While she was in hospital, the children visited her every day. In response to her constant fears and questions, they told her that they were happy and comfortable. They talked about the things they had done with their foster parents and of the places they had visited. They were missing her, of course, because they loved her, but they were still settled and they were together. To my surprise, Pam did not insist on leaving the hospital, but seemed happy to stay there for the time being.

One day she asked me to find out whether the children could stay with their foster parents indefinitely. The answer was an emphatic 'yes'. The foster parents had fallen in love with their new family and did not want to lose them. Pam died that day. She had, it seemed to me, defied medical science through willpower. She had held on to life simply in order to make sure that her children were going to be all right. Once her fears had been settled, she had let go of life and had succumbed to the cancer that should have taken her life months before.

I am not the only doctor to have noticed such cases. In recent years, doctors have described about 200 cases of regression of terminal cancer. In those cases, the patients did not just live on until they were ready to die, they inexplicably managed to defeat an apparently undefeatable

Every year, thousands of invalids make the pilgrimage to the shrine at Lourdes in hope of a cure. In this century, no less than 64 miraculous cures have been recorded, confounding those who doubt the strength of the mind and spirit. (See page 22).

cancer. In those 200 cases, the patients had been told that they would die, but they all lived and the cancer disappeared. How? There is no orthodox explanation for those recoveries, but both Norman Cousins and I believe that we can offer explanations.

onsider, too, what has happened at the shrine at Lourdes in France this century. Many doctors regard those who make a pilgrimage to Lourdes in the hope of a cure to be wasting their time. But most of those who make the effort really believe that they will get better. They are inspired by hope and faith. They go because they believe, in their hearts, that by going they will get better. So far this century, there have been no less than 64 fully documented miracles at Lourdes – including cases where apparently permanently withered limbs have regenerated.

Do not make the mistake of assuming that it is easy to experience a miracle at Lourdes. It is not. Before an official miracle can be listed, a number of strict conditions must be observed. First, the disease that has been cured must be serious, normally incurable and unlikely to have responded to treatment. Second, a disease which disappears must not have reached a state where it could have disappeared by itself. Third, no medication should have been given to the patient. Fourth, the cure must be sudden and reached more or less spontaneously. Finally, the cure must be complete. If the Medical Bureau at Lourdes (which consists of anything up to 100 doctors) decides that there is a possibility of a medically inexplicable cure, they open a dossier on the patient and invite him to return to Lourdes the following year. For at least three years, the pilgrim must return to Lourdes and be re-examined. Then, and only then, will the case be referred to the International Medical Committee at Lourdes. Only if the Committee is convinced that the cure has no medical explanation will the Church be invited to declare the healing a miracle.

An enormous amount of research has been done to investigate exactly *how* the mind can have such an extraordinary effect on the body. Most of the published papers have produced more questions than answers and have exposed more bewildering wonders of the human mind.

For example, have you ever noticed that if you are at a party where dozens of people are talking loudly and someone mentions your name, your ears will automatically prick up? You will have isolated the sounds of your name from the general hubbub, even though you had not consciously been listening to the conversation concerned.

From research done in the last few years, it seems that our hearing acuity is very much more powerful than any of us might have imagined. In one fascinating experiment, volunteers listened to a recording of various numbers being read out. Every time the number five was mentioned, a puff of air was blown on to the eyelids of the volunteers. Eventually, the individuals all acquired reflexes which meant that they blinked whenever they heard the number five on the tape.

That was all straightforward enough, but the next part of the experiment was remarkable. When the volume was turned down so that the voice on the tape was inaudible, the volunteers still blinked every time the number five was mentioned. Somehow, they had managed to hear unconsciously what they had been unable to detect consciously.

All this sounds more like science fiction or science fantasy than science fact, but countless scientists around the world are now prepared to confirm that the powers of the mind are far greater than most of us have ever imagined. Since Uri Geller startled the world with his metal-bending experiments, numerous researchers have done similar experiments with other individuals and have produced similar results. At London University's Birkbeck College, for example, Professor John Hasted has tested over 20 young people, using sophisticated electronic sensors to prevent trickery and to filter out the effects of freak atmospheric conditions and electrical interference. He, and other scientists around the world conducting similar experiments, have confirmed that many individuals do have quite remarkable and totally inexplicable powers. Cameramen working with film crews recording such experiments have reported that their equipment has frequently been broken or distorted.

Ordinary people, too, have provided plenty of food for thought. For example, in California, a 49-year-old widow suddenly woke up at two o'clock in the morning after dreaming of a burning house full of elderly people running about in their nightwear. The dream was so realistic that the woman felt that she had to do something about it. Feeling rather foolish, she dressed quickly and drove off to an old people's home that she helped to run, anxious to make sure that nothing was wrong. In a small room at the back of the house, she found flames shooting out of a gas main. No one had seen the fire and no one had called for help. The fire brigade chief who dealt with the blaze said that within another 30 minutes it would have destroyed the house and all the inhabitants.

Although no one can explain phenomena of this type, fewer and fewer scientists are now prepared to deny that they occur. Indeed, a growing number of scientists are beginning to investigate such abnormal powers. At the Maudsley Hospital in London, for example, Dr Peter Fenwick and his colleagues have found a significant number of head injuries, episodes of being knocked unconscious, blackouts and serious illnesses in the medical histories of the mediums they have studied. From their work it seems that there is a link between an individual being knocked unconscious and that individual later showing telepathic or clairvoyant skills.

It is right that we should still treat all such results with a healthy mixture of cynicism and scepticism, but I firmly believe that the evidence does now support the existence of extra-sensory perception, telepathy and premonitions. These sensuous feelings are as real as vision and hearing, and the capacities of the sensory organs which we have not yet identified are so vast that we cannot even define the boundaries with any confidence.

here is now a staggering amount of evidence available to show that the power of the mind can have a constructive and healing effect on the body. The very same powers that can stimulate the development of disease can be used to stimulate the body's self-healing processes. Many doctors believe in the power of the mind and use it themselves, even though they may be reluctant to share their feelings with their patients or their colleagues. For example, I know many doctors who used to take sleeping tablets when they were tired and under pressure. Today, however, they use the sort of techniques described in this book to help themselves relax and get to sleep.

When I was a medical student in the late 1960s, I was startled by the sight of a physiology lecturer pushing a metal spike into his biceps to show us the electrical effects produced by a muscle contracting. The lecturer used to do this as a regular part of his teaching course and he never bled or seemed to suffer any pain. The spike was about as long and as thick as a knitting needle and the lecturer would push it right into his arm without hesitating or flinching.

I was impressed by that memory for years but never really understood how the lecturer had done it. He had used the incident to demonstrate some minor aspect of human physiology. He had (presumably deliberately) failed to explain to us how he had managed to push a spike into his arm without feeling any pain. Then, fairly recently, I met an American doctor who had had a similar experience while still a medical student. His lecturer had also pushed a metal skewer about the length of a knitting needle straight through the centre of his biceps muscle, without losing one drop of blood and without suffering in any obvious way at all.

This student had asked his lecturer to explain how he managed to perform such a feat. The lecturer told him that, every time he performed the experiment, he would mentally place himself in a far corner at the back of the room so that he would not feel any pain as the spike went into his muscle, and he would leave behind instructions that his body's defences were to deal with any infection and ensure that there was no loss of blood. This was not some publicity-starved performer or masochistic lunatic. It was a sane, sensible, sober physiology lecturer at an American medical school. It illustrates the remarkable way in which the mind can influence the body.

One of the first properly organized scientific experiments to show the power of the mind took place in Australia in 1983. Researchers took a large group of people who had absolutely nothing in common apart from the fact that none of them had ever played basketball before. After being allowed to spend one day throwing basketballs through a hoop, the volunteers were divided into three groups.

The members of the first group were told not to play any basketball at all for a month. They were told not even to think about basketball. The people in the second group were told to practise every day for ten minutes at a time. The volunteers in the third group were told to spend ten minutes a day imagining that they were throwing balls into a basket.

One month later, the people in the first group were no better at basketball than they had been at the start of the whole exercise. However, the other two groups had improved by very similar amounts. The players who had been spending their time out on the court physically throwing basketballs through hoops had improved by 24 per cent; the players who had spent ten minutes a day imagining that they had been throwing basketballs through hoops had improved by 23 per cent.

Numerous other sportsmen have confirmed the value of using 'mindpower' in sport. Few people who saw him will forget the sight of Arthur Ashe meditating between points during one Wimbledon Final.

While the centre court crowd roared and cheered, Ashe sat quietly in his chair, closed his eyes and recharged his spiritual and mental batteries. Jack Nicklaus, one of the greatest golfers in our era, has admitted that he uses mental imagery to help improve his game. He 'sees' himself playing successful shots and feeds positive, winning images into his mind. In England, psychologists have been used to help top England batsman, David Gower, and his county cricket team, Leicestershire, employing the power of meditation to improve motivation, relaxation and concentration. Queens Park Rangers football team has used similar techniques.

In his book *Comeback: My Race For The America's Cup*, yachtsman Dennis Connor wrote that: 'Another part of the psychological build up had a lot to do with my theory that one's self-image cannot distinguish between reality and a very vivid imagination. I tried to get the guys to imagine how good it would feel to execute the perfect cast off or the perfect jibe. I asked them to imagine what it would be like to perform to complete perfection. I told them to capture the images of that perfection in their mind's eye. I asked them to use their affirmations to raise their self-image in the same way that they used real-life experiences to shape their own image of themselves. If you can visualize something, you can actualize it.'

Connor's brave honesty (not many macho sportsmen would admit that they used such techniques to help them win) illustrates the remarkable effect that ordinary sportsmen and sportswomen can expect if they, too, use mental imagery. The sportsman who has faith and who ignores criticism (including his own) will always do far better than the one who spends his time worrying about what can go wrong. By using the power of the mind properly, you can increase your chances of winning.

Champion golfer Jack Nicklaus envisages himself playing winning shots to improve his performance.

There cannot be a more 'mechanical' sport than Grand Prix motor car racing, where drivers regularly risk their lives driving cars around twisting and turning tracks at 200 mph. Yet even Grand Prix drivers admit that mental power and mental imagery play an important part in their success. Nigel Mansell, the most successful British Grand Prix driver of the 1980s, admits that he only really began to drive successfully when he found himself visualizing his car starting to leave a bend on the track before it had even entered it. Top, world-class drivers admit that their minds switch into a special slow-motion style during a race. Each moment lasts a small lifetime and the driver distances himself from the reality of the race in order to plan his actions coolly and dispassionately. Anyone who has ever been in a car crash will know what they mean: the few seconds before the impact seem to last an eternity.

On pages 134 to 135 I have explained in detail how any sportsperson can improve his or her game by using tricks of mind over body.

ven more impressive than any of the exploits of our leading sports stars has been the work done in America by Dr Carl Simonton and his wife. For a number of years, they have been teaching patients how to cope with cancer by using their imaginations. The theory is that if the imagination can have a destructive effect, it can also have a positive one. If people can give themselves cancer by negative thinking, they should be able to protect themselves against it and maybe even cure themselves of it by positive thinking. In the first years of their experimental work, the

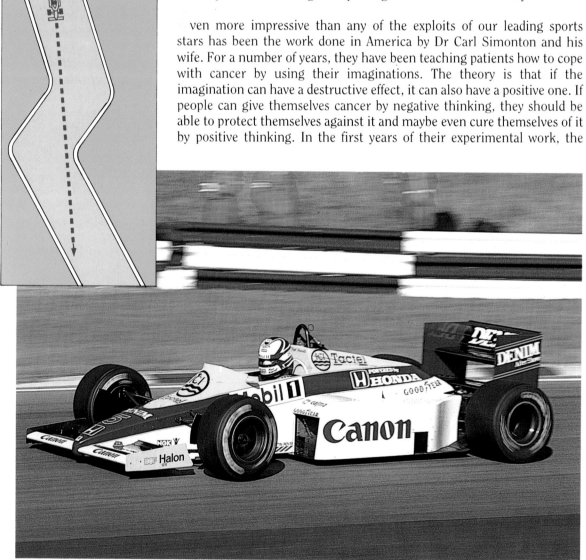

Nigel Mansell became a more successful racing driver when he began to visualize himself driving well ahead of the track immediately before him. This increased his sense of control over the race.

Simontons have found that their patients have lived, on average, more than a year longer than other patients who were not encouraged to use their minds to help fight their disease.

All around the world, doctors are now beginning to come up with similarly impressive results, often being able to show that the state of the patient's mind and his expectations can have just as important an effect on his progress as the type of treatment he is offered.

There have even been papers showing that the attitude a doctor takes towards his patients will also have a powerful effect on the patient's chances of recovering. For example, in May 1987, the *British Medical Journal* published a paper in which a general practitioner working in Southampton described the difference the doctor's attitude made to a patient's chances of getting better. For his research project, Dr K.B. Thomas took a group of 200 patients who were seeking advice from a general practitioner. None of the patients had any abnormal physical signs and in none of the patients was any specific, definite diagnosis made.

The patients were then randomly selected for one of four different types of consultation. The first group was given treatment and what Thomas called a consultation in a positive manner. The second group was given no treatment but was given encouragement and the positive-manner consultation. The third group was given treatment and a consultation in a negative manner. The fourth group was given no treatment and no encouragement – the patients were given only a consultation in a negative manner.

In positive-manner consultations, the patient was told firmly that he would be better in a few days. In negative-manner consultations, the patient was told, 'I cannot be certain what is the matter with you'. The treatment given was a vitamin tablet prescribed as a placebo, simply to make the patient think that he was being prescribed something useful.

The results were impressive. Thomas found that giving the patient treatment made very little difference to his chances of feeling better. However, he did find that the patients who had had a positive-manner consultation got better much quicker than the patients who had had a negative-manner consultation. Two weeks after the consultation, only 39 per cent of the patients who had had the negative-manner consultation felt better, whereas 64 per cent of the patients who had had the positive-manner consultation felt better.

strongly suspect that, within the next few years, many similar papers will be published in other medical journals. Doctors will, at last, be able to prove what many of us have suspected for a long time – that the doctor who offers hope, reassurance and positive, helpful advice will have a much higher healing rate than the doctor who cares little and who merely dishes out pills. Caring is, it seems, part of the curing process.

Meanwhile, while we wait for the medical establishment to accept what common sense has for a long time hinted at and what science now indicates is the truth, there are many ways in which we can all use the power of our minds to help us stay healthy and to help us become well again when we fall ill. The rest of this book describes the many practical ways in which you can use your mind to help your body.

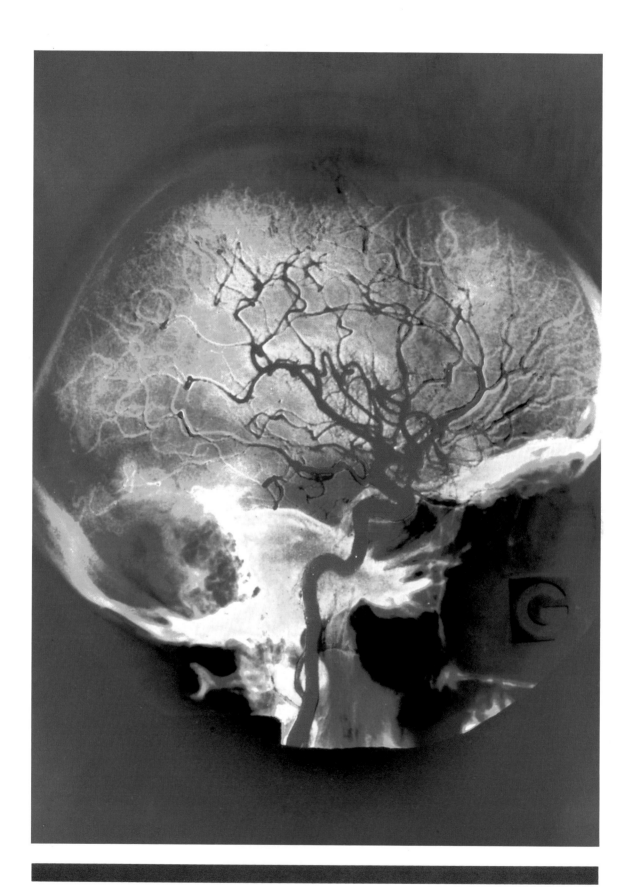

1

Know Your Own Mind

The key to health and happiness lies in the complex and colourful workings of the individual mind. The human skull shelters this impressive and organic machine, which governs all the vagaries of human behaviour.

Have you ever wondered why different people suffer from different diseases when exposed to exactly the same problems and pressures? One man who is worried about his job will develop high blood pressure, another, with exactly the same anxiety, will develop an ulcer, a third will have asthma and a fourth will remain perfectly fit and healthy, however much stress and pressure he is exposed to! Faced with almost identical problems, one woman will develop colitis, another will acquire a heart problem and a third will suffer from eczema.

It is now known that the reason for these variations lies within the individual personalities of the people concerned. The personality of any individual has a significant effect on the type of disorder from which he or she is most likely to suffer. The personality does not just have a tremendous influence on the way an individual's body responds to stress, pressure and environmental problems; it also has an effect on the type of illness he or she subsequently develops.

The importance of this particular relationship lies, of course, in the fact that, by understanding a little more about your own personality, you will be able to tell what sort of problems you are most likely to face and you can then be better aware of the early warning signs. If you have ever built a sandcastle and then struggled to find the weak patches and spot the cracks in the walls as they appear, you will know that an understanding of your own psychological weaknesses – and strengths – will be invaluable when it comes to fighting off illness.

Some of the evidence linking personality type to specific kinds of disease is very old. In 1910, William Osler wrote in *The Lancet* that it was ambitious, hard-working men who were most likely to develop heart trouble. In 1945, another researcher suggested that people who have heart attacks are often tortured by their need to compete with their fathers. Since then a huge number of researchers have managed to amplify both these statements. For example, in her book, *Biotypes*, Joan Arehart-Treichel tells how, in the early 1950s, an upholsterer repairing chairs in a reception room shared by two doctors noticed that only the front edges of the chairs were worn – as though the patients who had been sitting there had been literally 'on edge'. The two doctors, Rosenman and

Friedman, spent a large part of the next two decades trying to find out more about the type of patient likely to have a heart attack.

When they published their discoveries in the early 1970s, they reported that the sort of person who gets a heart attack is usually male and commonly under a tremendous amount of pressure. Even today, although many women have responsible, stressful positions in Government, industry and other professions, men frequently suffer from heart attacks more than women. This is often because they deliberately suppress their emotions and do not allow themselves to express their feelings. Rosenman and Friedman also managed to show that men who are susceptible to heart attacks invariably have a particularly strong drive to compete and to achieve. They are, reported the doctors, competitive, aggressive, short-tempered, impatient, easily frustrated, almost always under pressure and angrily ever-determined to achieve great things. The potential heart attack patient, it seems, works long hours, sets out to succeed, finds it difficult to sit still, is usually unable to relax and is a perfectionist. No matter how successful this person is, he will rarely be able to satisfy his ambitions. And, of course, it is not how successful you actually are that determines your sense of personal satisfaction, it is how successful you think you are.

Evidence linking personality to cancer goes back a long way – further than the evidence linking personality to heart disease. In the second century AD, the Roman physician, Galen, noticed that women who are depressed are far more likely to develop cancer than women who are happy.

In recent years, we have acquired a considerable amount of information to support and complement that early observation. Caroline Thomas and Karen Duszynski of Johns Hopkins School of Medicine were able to show that there was a significant psychological similarity between those medical students who later developed malignant tumours. The students who developed cancer all seemed to share a feeling, at a fairly early age, that they were not close to their parents. Often the person who develops cancer has had an unhappy childhood. This may have been because his or her parents were divorced, or perhaps because one parent has died or even simply because his or her parents never showed him or her much love or affection. To get the love he or she missed as a child, such an individual strives too hard to please others. He or she grows up suffering from a lack of love, a sense of loneliness and a feeling that he or she has been deserted by those closest to him or her.

Typically, on getting any positive feedback – either through personal success or through the love of a friend or partner – such a person tends to regard the source of that feedback as vitally important. If the career success fades or the relationship breaks up, the man or woman with a cancer-prone personality will relapse into a lonely, anxious, hopeless individual. The bitterness and despair such people feel can in itself result in the development of a life-threatening cancer. Cancer victims tend to give more than they take; they tend to repress their own desires and their own emotional feelings. Unselfishly, they will always do their best to please those around them. When anything goes wrong with the world they have created for themselves, they develop cancer. Incidentally, it has been suggested that women who breast-feed are less likely to get cancer of the breast because of some aspect of the feeding process. Could it be, I wonder, that the sort of generous, open, loving women who choose to breast-feed are simply not the sort of women who are particularly likely to develop cancer anyway?

There is evidence showing that it is possible to link specific personality types to all sorts of diseases. There is, for example, even evidence to show that personality factors determine which people are most likely to suffer from common colds and minor throat and chest infections. Dr Richard Totman of Sussex University and Dr Donald Broadbent of Oxford University, working with the Common Cold Research Unit in England, have come to the conclusion that introverts are far more likely to get lots of colds than extroverts. Further information suggests that people who are obsessional are particularly likely to get colds. It seems, too, that the severity of the symptoms endured by someone who has a cold depends very largely upon the amount of stress and strain he thinks he is under at the time.

As I have already pointed out, I do not expect many readers to be able to recognize themselves from the very specific, one-dimensional pen portraits given here, but these personality types do exist and are significant. It is, of course, important to remember that specific types of personality are not only linked to specific physical conditions, but that there is also a great deal of evidence showing that the personality of an individual will have an influence on the life-style he adopts, the type of partner he chooses and the sort of work he undertakes. Clearly, therefore, any individual's personality will help to ensure that his life follows a certain, well-defined pattern – and, inevitably, that he comes face to face with a series of stresses and problems.

Our personalities play a vitally important part in our lives. They determine the sort of immediate environment we create for ourselves and they then determine the way in which we respond to that environment – and to the stresses and strains that are inherent in that self-made environment. It is our minds which commonly kill our bodies, but it is our personalities which decide exactly how the killing is to be done.

If you are to use your mind to control your body – and your life – then it is important that you understand as much as possible about your own personality. Answer the quizzes that follow and you will learn a great deal about yourself! You will also learn a great deal about how your own personality influences your relationship with others. Remember that just as your personality has many different facets, so do the personalities of the people you love and work with. Personal relationships are a major potential cause of stress. It is your relationships with other people which commonly bring happiness, sadness and many other emotions into your life.

The quizzes that follow will help you understand yourself more thoroughly and, by understanding yourself, you will be far better equipped to ensure that your relationships with friends, partners and strangers are, as far as possible, free from tension and anxiety. You will, I hope, enjoy learning more about yourself, but this chapter is not just here for fun. If you work your way through the quizzes carefully and honestly, your mental and physical health will benefit enormously.

*P*ersonality and *I*llness *P*rofiles

The pen portraits below are not exhaustive, but they are based on sound clinical work which has been done around the world. They are included here, not because many readers will necessarily be able to identify instantly with the types outlined (relatively few people fit neatly into one rigid personality compartment), but because the evidence linking these extreme

The stiff upper lip type	If you usually try to hide the way you feel – whether you are sad, happy or angry – you are likely to end up suffering from an allergy problem, such as asthma or eczema.
The shy, self-effacing type	In 1965, R.H. Moos and G.F. Solomon published a survey suggesting that patients suffering from rheumatoid arthritis tend to be martyrs, self-conscious, shy, intolerant of anything second-rate, inhibited, tense, nervous, moody, unable to express their anger, convinced that their mothers rejected them and that their fathers were too strict. The arthritis sufferer often feels inferior and inadequate.
The neat, orderly, efficient type	Are you a perfectionist always keen to do things absolutely right? If so, you are likely to get headaches – particularly migraine headaches.
The intolerant, humourless, rather rigid type	If you have difficulty in adapting to change and you rarely see the funny side when things go wrong, it is possible that you could end up suffering from depressive illness.

personality types to corresponding kinds of illness is powerful. Be careful not to draw wrong conclusions about others – and if you draw negative conclusions, keep them to yourself!

The anxious-for-lots-of-love type	Do you like being mothered? Do you always feel the need to be loved? If so, you are the type to suffer from indigestion – and eventually, perhaps, a stomach ulcer.
The aggressive, impatient, ambitious type	The more competitive you are and the harder you push yourself, the more likely you are to have a heart attack.
The indecisive, immature, obsessive type	In 1955, G.L. Engel published a study suggesting that patients suffering from colitis tended to be obsessive, compulsive, indecisive, morally rigid, over-intellectual, conforming and anxious – desperate to be considered 'normal' and 'average' by their peers. Colitis sufferers are also said to be exceptionally touchy and to burst into tears often.
The 'please everyone' type	If you are always trying too hard – always doing what other people want and never doing what you want – you need to watch out for early signs of cancer. If you were more selfish, you would probably be healthier.

What Makes You Tick?

The quizzes are divided into three groups. First, there are 60 questions designed to help you find out some basic facts about your personality. Second, there is a series of short quizzes to help you find out why you do the things you do – what sort of driving forces control your behaviour. Third, there are some short quizzes designed to help you understand how your behaviour changes when you are with other people. Later in the book are quizzes and tests designed to help you improve your ability to use your mental powers. The questions in this chapter are designed solely to help you understand yourself a little better.

You cannot, of course, completely change your personality! You cannot wake up one morning as an obsessive individual with absolutely no self confidence and go to bed the same day unconcerned, disorganized and bursting with confidence in yourself and your own abilities! But, by learning as much as you can about your weaknesses and your strengths, you will be able to help yourself a great deal.

Few things will help you deal with life more effectively than understanding your weak points. For example, imagine that you find it difficult to relax, that you are naturally tense and that you respond badly to new stresses. If you do not understand this weakness, the chances are that your health will suffer in many ways. You will be more likely to suffer from the physical disorders which are known to be associated with stress and pressure – and with an inability to relax. You will be more susceptible to heart disease, high blood pressure, respiratory and other damaging disorders varying from headaches to eczema. You will probably find it difficult to get to sleep at night. When pressures pile up, you may become irritable and edgy. You may well panic easily and have difficulty in making important decisions when you are threatened.

Inevitably, your relationships will suffer. At home you will shout at those you love for no good reason. At work you will make more mistakes. But once you *know* that one of your natural weaknesses is an inability to relax, you can make an effort to deal with it. You can learn how to relax your body and your mind – and how to cope when things go wrong. By recognizing the early signs which warn you that your weakness is beginning to show, you can start to see yourself as other people see you! Meanwhile your basic personality will not have changed at all: you will simply have learned to cope with your weaknesses effectively and permanently.

A word of warning: remember that these preliminary questionnaires are designed simply to give you a rough idea of the sort of person you are. Remember, too, that you would not be human if you did not find flaws in your emotional make-up. Much of the rest of this book is designed to help you overcome those weaknesses and take full advantage of your strengths. Finally, there are no 'right' or 'wrong' answers to any of these questions. To obtain useful results, you must answer every question as honestly as you possibly can, not the way you think you should – and do not spend too long working out the best answers – just answer the way you feel!

*K*now *Y*our *P*ersonality

This special quiz will help you find out exactly how your personality is affecting your life. Answer each question carefully and honestly, and keep a record of all your 'YES' answers on the scoreboard below. Put a pencil tick in the appropriate squares as you work your way through the questions. So, for example, if you answer 'YES' to question 1, you should tick the first box in the 'B' column. If you answer 'YES' to question 2, you should tick the first box in the 'A' column. Your score for each letter should remain within the shaded areas. If your score takes you outside the shaded area, you should consult the advice section on page 37.

A	B	C	D	E	F

yes

1 Do you ever go through a day without touching someone you love at least once?   **B**

2 Do you find it difficult to laugh at yourself?   **A**

3 Do you think that crying is usually a sign of weakness?   **C**

4 Do you dislike physical signs of affection?   **B**

5 Would you try to hold back your tears if attending a funeral or some other sad event?   **C**

6 Would you pretend that you had something in your eye if you were unexpectedly discovered crying?   **C**

7 Do you usually avoid doing things that might upset other people, even if they are things that you would like to do?   **E**

8 Do you become cross if you are in an important meeting and someone starts to tell a joke or funny story?   **A**

9 Would you be deeply offended if you did something silly and people laughed at you?   **A**

10 Do you rarely tell those you love just how you feel about them?   **B**

11 Do you feel guilty if you cry in public?   **C**

12 Do you think that boys should be encouraged to hide their tears?   **C**

13 Do you feel bad if you go into a shop and come out without having bought anything?   **E**

14 Do you get irritated easily?   **F**

15 Do you ever suffer from panic attacks?   **F**

16 Do you invariably dress to please other people?   **E**

17 Do you dislike being kissed and hugged by people you love?   **B**

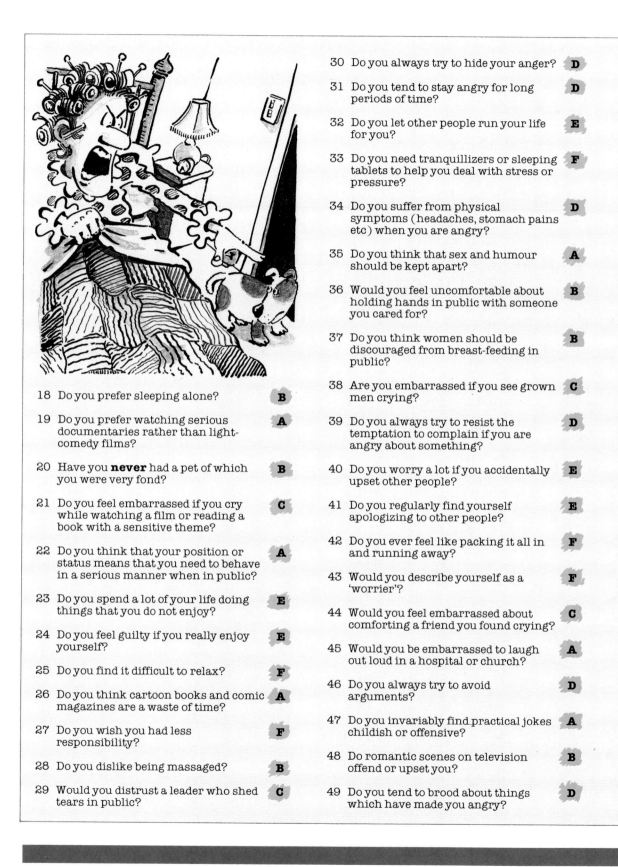

18 Do you prefer sleeping alone? **B**

19 Do you prefer watching serious documentaries rather than light-comedy films? **A**

20 Have you **never** had a pet of which you were very fond? **B**

21 Do you feel embarrassed if you cry while watching a film or reading a book with a sensitive theme? **C**

22 Do you think that your position or status means that you need to behave in a serious manner when in public? **A**

23 Do you spend a lot of your life doing things that you do not enjoy? **E**

24 Do you feel guilty if you really enjoy yourself? **E**

25 Do you find it difficult to relax? **F**

26 Do you think cartoon books and comic magazines are a waste of time? **A**

27 Do you wish you had less responsibility? **F**

28 Do you dislike being massaged? **B**

29 Would you distrust a leader who shed tears in public? **C**

30 Do you always try to hide your anger? **D**

31 Do you tend to stay angry for long periods of time? **D**

32 Do you let other people run your life for you? **E**

33 Do you need tranquillizers or sleeping tablets to help you deal with stress or pressure? **F**

34 Do you suffer from physical symptoms (headaches, stomach pains etc) when you are angry? **D**

35 Do you think that sex and humour should be kept apart? **A**

36 Would you feel uncomfortable about holding hands in public with someone you cared for? **B**

37 Do you think women should be discouraged from breast-feeding in public? **B**

38 Are you embarrassed if you see grown men crying? **C**

39 Do you always try to resist the temptation to complain if you are angry about something? **D**

40 Do you worry a lot if you accidentally upset other people? **E**

41 Do you regularly find yourself apologizing to other people? **E**

42 Do you ever feel like packing it all in and running away? **F**

43 Would you describe yourself as a 'worrier'? **F**

44 Would you feel embarrassed about comforting a friend you found crying? **C**

45 Would you be embarrassed to laugh out loud in a hospital or church? **A**

46 Do you always try to avoid arguments? **D**

47 Do you invariably find practical jokes childish or offensive? **A**

48 Do romantic scenes on television offend or upset you? **B**

49 Do you tend to brood about things which have made you angry? **D**

50 Do you have difficulty in getting to sleep after something has annoyed you? **D**

51 Do you often find yourself wishing that you had more skills and talents? **E**

52 Do you always seem to be in a hurry? **F**

53 Do you think that time spent laughing is time wasted? **A**

54 Do you think that tears are an unnecessary expression of emotion? **C**

55 Does your face ever go red (or white) when you get angry? **D**

56 Do you suffer from any symptoms which are caused or made worse by pressure? **F**

57 Do you think you have far more weaknesses than strengths? **E**

58 Have you ever got into trouble because of your anger? **D**

59 Does your temper ever get out of control? **D**

60 Do you find yourself frequently feeling frustrated? **F**

If you scored more than 4 'A' answers

There is too little laughter in your life. Laughter is not just a pleasant experience, it is a positive natural phenomenon that will help you stay healthy. Laughter helps by improving respiration, lowering blood pressure and 'tuning' your heart. To find out more about laughter's beneficial effects and to discover how to put more laughter into your life you should read pages 78 to 80.

If you scored more than 5 'B' answers

You are too cool, detached and unemotional. You will live longer and be healthier if you allow yourself to show how you feel. To find out more — and to discover how to be less cool and detached — see pages 82 to 83.

If you scored more than 2 'C' answers

Your attitude towards crying is not healthy. Crying is a natural human way of responding to sadness. Crying is nothing to feel ashamed of — see pages 72 to 73.

If you scored more than 3 'D' answers

Anger is a killer — and could be damaging your health. Diseases such as high blood pressure and strokes can be caused by anger. See page 75 for advice.

If you scored more than 2 'E' answers

You need to be more self-confident. A lack of self-confidence can be destructive. To find out how to build up your self-confidence, turn to pages 84 to 85.

If you scored more than 3 'F' answers

You need to relax more and calm down a little. Tension is building up and may be threatening your health. You will find details about how to relax efficiently and effectively on pages 89 to 101.

Why Do You Do the Things You Do?

What makes people continue with jobs they hate? Why do men and women throw themselves into disastrous affairs? What makes us worry about what other people think of us? Most of the things we do are a result of our responses to a series of fundamental driving forces. We behave according to these forces and our lives are governed by them. It is these forces which determine the priorities in our lives.

Traditionally, influences which affect human behaviour are divided into the seven virtues – prudence, temperance, fortitude, justice, faith, hope and love – and the seven sins – pride, covetousness, lust, envy, gluttony, anger and sloth. However, life is not quite as black and white as this simple division into virtues and sins might suggest. There are times when prudence (normally considered a virtue) could be regarded as more sinful than pride (normally thought of as a sin). People who are too prudent can appear grasping and mean-spirited. Individuals who have no pride can become slovenly, careless, thoughtless and inefficient.

Any attempt to study human behaviour – why we do the things we do – is made even more complicated by the fact that things are never quite as simple as they may appear to be. There is, for example, nearly always some selfish, self-satisfying motive behind every good deed.

The voluntary worker who spends several hours every week helping the elderly, the sick or the disabled is in fact satisfying his or her own urges and needs just as much as he or she is satisfying the needs of the elderly, the sick or the disabled. Dedicating hours of his or her life to helping others, he or she may be driven by a desperate need to be loved, admired and respected. He or she may be lonely, with few friends, have too much time and too little to do. He or she might well be gaining just as much from helping others as those being given support, and may, perhaps, be struggling to escape from boredom or a sense of worthlessness. Good deeds which are partly or wholly built on selfish motives are not, of course, of any less value because of it. The person who is being helped still benefits.

If we are to understand ourselves – and those with whom we live and work – we have to accept that there are very few downright sinful driving forces. Just about any one of the basic driving forces I have defined can produce bad deeds as easily as good deeds. Vanity can make someone self-centred and uncaring but it can also produce thoughtful, careful and considerate behaviour. Fear can inspire loyalty and selflessness as easily as it can inspire cowardice. Traitors and heroes alike are often driven by fear. Aggression can turn a man or a woman into a bully or a saviour. Ambition can lead to success and happiness or dismay and depression.

In the end it is, perhaps, what you do that matters and not why you do it. But understanding why you – and those around you – do the things you do will help you to enjoy a happier and more satisfying life.

The quizzes that follow are designed to help you find out which of these forces have the greatest impact on your life. Look at the areas where you score highest to find the most important forces in your life.

Openness

1 How many times have you spoken to strangers on trains?

(a) never
(b) occasionally
(c) quite often

2 How many friends and acquaintances have you got?

(a) a lot
(b) quite a few
(c) hardly any

3 Do you make friends easily?

(a) yes
(b) no

4 Which do you prefer?

(a) noisy evenings with lots of people
(b) very quiet evenings, alone or with one person
(c) a mixture – depending on your mood

5 How often do you go to parties?

(a) hardly ever
(b) occasionally
(c) frequently

6 How many of your neighbours do you know by their first names?

(a) none or hardly any
(b) all or most of them
(c) somewhere in between the two

7 Do you like travelling and meeting people?

(a) yes – definitely
(b) sometimes
(c) no – definitely not

8 You are going on holiday. Which do you prefer?

(a) somewhere with lots of bright lights and busy beaches
(b) somewhere quiet and peaceful
(c) somewhere in between those two extremes

9 Do you like being the centre of attention?

(a) yes
(b) no

10 Would you like to be famous? Would you like to be recognized in the street?

(a) yes
(b) no

Optimism

1 You have enjoyed half a bottle of wine. Would you describe the bottle as:

   (a) half full?
   (b) half empty?

2 Do you bet?

   (a) occasionally
   (b) often
   (c) never

3 Do you think the future is:

   (a) rosy – full of better things?
   (b) black and full of sadness?
   (c) going to be a mixture of good and bad times?

4 Do you think that most people are:

   (a) basically honest?
   (b) basically dishonest?
   (c) a bit of both?

5 How big a portion of your income do you spend on insurance?

   (a) hardly anything – probably less than most people
   (b) a lot – probably more than most people
   (c) about the same as most people

6 Do you dream about what you would do if you won a lot of money?

   (a) often
   (b) occasionally
   (c) never

7 When you start something new do you usually feel:

   (a) excited and enthusiastic?
   (b) a mixture of emotions?
   (c) very anxious – worrying about what could go wrong?

8 If the postman brings an unexpected parcel do you feel:

   (a) thrilled – assuming it is something good?
   (b) merely curious?
   (c) worried – assuming it is a problem?

9 How do you deal with money?

   (a) save as much as you can for a rainy day
   (b) save a little
   (c) spend everything – let tomorrow look after itself

10 Which of these phrases describes you best?

   (a) you look before you leap
   (b) you tend to jump in with both feet
   (c) you like to dip your toe in the water first

Vanity

1 You are buying jeans. Would you pay more for a designer label if you were convinced that you could buy similar quality for a lower price?

   (a) yes
   (b) no

2 You are going out to dinner. You notice a spot on your nose. Do you:

   (a) ignore it?
   (b) refuse to go out?
   (c) do your best to cover it up but probably worry about it all evening?

3 Someone mentions a writer you have never heard of. Do you:

   (a) pretend to know what he is talking about and hope you are not found out?
   (b) admit that you have never heard of the writer concerned?
   (c) try to change the subject quickly?

4 Do you worry about your appearance?

   (a) occasionally
   (b) all the time
   (c) hardly ever

5 Someone tells you that a favourite jacket does not suit you. Do you:

   (a) wear it anyway and take no notice?
   (b) wear it occasionally but always feel uncomfortable?
   (c) never wear it again?

6 You have a small, battered car and you are attending a function where everyone else will turn up in expensive, polished limousines. Do you:

(a) *still drive up to the front door and park your car anywhere convenient?*
(b) *use your own car but park around the corner and hope that no one sees you arrive?*
(c) *use a taxi or hire car for the evening?*

7 If you are visiting a hairdresser do you:

(a) *spend some time explaining exactly what you want?*
(b) *mutter some quick instructions and then let the hairdresser get on with it?*
(c) *sit down and just hope it is all over quickly?*

8 You are invited to join a pseudo academic organization. For a small fee, you can have letters after your name. Would you:

(a) *join, use the qualifications and pretend that they are genuine?*
(b) *think about it first?*
(c) *turn down the invitation without a second thought?*

9 If you found a safe, reliable practitioner and you had the money to spend, would you ever have plastic surgery to improve your appearance?

(a) *yes*
(b) *no*

10 Do you ever wear clothes because they show off your figure?

(a) *never*
(b) *occasionally*
(c) *often*

*R*omanticism

1 Do you like buying or receiving flowers?

(a) *yes*
(b) *no*

2 Which would you prefer?

(a) *an evening with friends – a real party?*
(b) *a quiet candlelit dinner for two in a country restaurant – with someone you love?*

3 Do you know the colour of your first lover's eyes?

(a) *yes*
(b) *no*

4 Do you carry a photograph of anyone with you in your wallet or handbag?

(a) *yes*
(b) *no*

5 Can you remember your first ever kiss?

(a) *yes*
(b) *no*

6 Do you believe in love at first sight?

(a) *yes*
(b) *no*

7 Do you enjoy flirting – or being flirted with?

(a) *yes*
(b) *no*

8 Do you ever have fantastic daydreams about possible relationships with film stars etc?

(a) *yes*
(b) *no*

9 Do you like holding hands with someone you love?

(a) *yes*
(b) *no*

10 You have just got married. You can afford a new cooker or a honeymoon. Which would you choose?

(a) *the cooker*
(b) *the honeymoon*

Aggression

1 If you got bad service in a restaurant would you:

   (a) complain loudly?
   (b) make a quiet protest?
   (c) say nothing?

2 How much time do you spend writing letters of complaint?

   (a) a lot
   (b) none at all
   (c) a little

3 Do you send or take back faulty items?

   (a) only very occasionally
   (b) sometimes – quite often
   (c) never

4 You order wine in a restaurant. It tastes horrible. Would you:

   (a) drink it and say nothing?
   (b) leave it but say nothing?
   (c) send it back and insist on a replacement?

5 You are waiting for service in a shop. The assistants are all gossiping. Would you:

   (a) wait until one of them sees you and serves you?
   (b) quietly try to catch their attention?
   (c) speak up loudly and demand attention?

6 A motorist nearly crashes into you. Would you:

   (a) quietly give thanks that he missed?
   (b) curse silently or privately?
   (c) chase after him, take his number or make a rude sign?

7 Would you argue with a policeman?

   (a) never
   (b) maybe – if really pushed
   (c) quite readily

8 How many times have you been in a fight?

   (a) never
   (b) once or twice at most
   (c) quite often or frequently

9 A workman makes a mess in your house. Would you:

   (a) clean it up and say nothing?
   (b) ask him to clean it up?
   (c) insist on him cleaning it up and complain to his boss?

10 If you thought your bank had made a mistake would you:

   (a) complain immediately?
   (b) check very carefully and then timidly ask if there could be an error?
   (c) say nothing and try to forget it?

Fear

1 Do your money problems keep you awake?

   (a) occasionally
   (b) often
   (c) never

2 If you read that your favourite food caused cancer in rats would you:

   (a) give it up immediately and prepare for the worst?
   (b) ignore the report and keep on eating your favourite food?
   (c) try to cut down a bit?

3 You get a note to telephone your doctor. Do you:

   (a) panic, telephone straight away and convince yourself that it will be bad news?
   (b) probably forget to call?
   (c) assume it is some routine reminder and telephone when you can?

4 Do you check that your doors and windows are locked:

   (a) when you remember – which is not all that often?
   (b) regularly each evening?
   (c) often more than once each evening?

5 If you had money and space to build a nuclear bomb-proof shelter in your garden would you:

   (a) probably build a swimming pool instead?
   (b) build the bomb-shelter as soon as possible?
   (c) want some time to think about it first?

6 If you thought your boss was behaving unreasonably would you:

(a) tell him/her regardless of the consequences?
(b) try and work out a way to tell him/her without offending him/her?
(c) keep quiet?

7 It is late at night and you have got to get home. Would you:

(a) use public transport happily?
(b) use public transport but be a nervous wreck by the time you got home?
(c) take a taxi even if you could not afford it?

8 You are lying awake in bed and you hear a creaking noise. Would you:

(a) go and see what it was?
(b) stay where you are, absolutely terrified?
(c) assume it is the heating pipes or the cat and go off to sleep?

9 Someone pushes in front of you in a queue. Would you:

(a) say nothing?
(b) say something regardless of his/her size and appearance?
(c) say something if you did not think you would be attacked?

10 Do you worry about your health?

(a) rarely
(b) occasionally
(c) most of the time

Obsessiveness

1 If you walk into a room and see a picture hanging off-centre do you:

(a) have to put it straight?
(b) want to put it straight – but stop yourself?
(c) ignore it – probably do not even notice it?

2 Do you think cars should be:

(a) washed regularly – once a week or so?
(b) washed occasionally when they are really dirty?
(c) washed only just before being sold?

3 Do you prefer to get the washing up done straight after a meal?

(a) yes
(b) no

4 Would you get upset if a visitor repeatedly made a mess in your home?

(a) yes
(b) no

5 Do you like to tidy up before going to bed?

(a) yes, always
(b) usually
(c) no, hardly ever

6 Do you always know how much money you have got in your pocket or purse?

(a) yes, exactly
(b) roughly
(c) no idea

7 Do you ever forget birthdays, anniversaries or appointments?

(a) yes, often
(b) no never
(c) yes, occasionally

8 Would you describe yourself as:

(a) very neat and tidy?
(b) fairly neat?
(c) very untidy – scruffy in your habits?

9 Do you get annoyed if other people borrow your things and fail to put them back in the correct place?

(a) yes
(b) no

10 Do you have lots of habits and a fairly strict daily routine?

(a) yes
(b) no

Lust

1 Do you have secret sexual fantasies?

   (a) occasionally
   (b) never
   (c) often

2 Do you think that you could have a purely platonic friendship with a member of the opposite sex?

   (a) yes
   (b) no

3 You are attracted to your partner's best friend. He/she makes a pass. Would you:

   (a) reluctantly refuse?
   (b) pause, think hard, but give in anyway?
   (c) accept the offer instantly?

4 Could you enjoy sex without love?

   (a) certainly
   (b) maybe
   (c) never

5 How often have you made love on a first date?

   (a) once
   (b) more than once
   (c) never

6 Do you think that sexual harassment at work should be:

   (a) regarded as inevitable, good fun and a bit of a joke?
   (b) stopped if possible but not taken too seriously?
   (c) stamped out?

7 What are your views on dirty magazines/blue movies?

   (a) approve wholeheartedly – enjoy them
   (b) will sneak a look when you can – find them quite exciting
   (c) disapprove

8 When you are dressing for a party, what is most important?

   (a) to look neat and smart
   (b) to wear something new and expensive looking
   (c) to look sexy

9 Do you think that any sexual acts between consenting adults should be illegal?

   (a) yes, definitely
   (b) maybe
   (c) no, definitely not

10 Do you look at strangers in the street and wonder what they are like naked or in bed?

   (a) never
   (b) sometimes
   (c) frequently

Ambition

1 If you had an opportunity to make a fortune by investing in a new business would you:

   (a) put in everything you could afford to lose?
   (b) prefer to pass up the opportunity and keep your savings safe?
   (c) invest everything you could lay your hands on?

2 Do you feel that you will:

   (a) never amount to anything very much?
   (b) one day become extremely important, powerful and successful?
   (c) do the best you can with your natural talents?

3 If you were applying for a new job, what would you consider most important?

   (a) possibilities for advancement and promotion
   (b) fringe benefits
   (c) pension plans

4 Do you work at night and weekends?

   (a) occasionally
   (b) never
   (c) frequently

5 Are most of your personal friends people you know through work?

   (a) yes
   (b) no

6 If your boss made it clear that he/she was attracted to you, would you:

   (a) try to keep the relationship on a professional footing?

(b) allow things to develop only if you found him/her attractive?

(c) use the opportunity to get ahead?

7 You are about to accept a new job. Then you discover that it will mean working away from home over Christmas. Would you:

(a) refuse outright?
(b) still accept?
(c) need time to think about it and talk it over with your family?

8 You discover a safe way to make money dishonestly. Would you:

(a) take the opportunity?
(b) inform the relevant authorities?
(c) think about it and probably do nothing?

9 Next Saturday afternoon there are two engagements you should attend: your daughter's school sports day and a business meeting. Would you:

(a) go to your daughter's school sports day?
(b) go to the business meeting?

10 When you are playing a game do you:

(a) play purely for fun and pleasure – you do not care if you win or lose?
(b) always play to win?
(c) play for fun but like to win?

Snobbishness

1 Do you ever wish you had had a better education?

(a) yes
(b) no

2 Do you ever feel ashamed of your accent?

(a) never
(b) occasionally
(c) often

3 Do you peek at the labels in other people's clothes or on their luggage?

(a) often
(b) sometimes
(c) never

4 If you were working around the house in old clothes and you had to go into town to buy something would you get changed first?

(a) certainly or almost certainly
(b) maybe
(c) no, definitely not

5 Do you name drop?

(a) never
(b) occasionally
(c) often

6 Do you ever secretly feel ashamed of your background or parents?

(a) yes, quite frequently
(b) yes, occasionally
(c) no, never

7 How would you treat a Duke if you met one at a party?

(a) the same as everyone else
(b) with a little extra respect
(c) with great respect

8 Do you put on a slightly posher voice when answering the telephone?

(a) never
(b) occasionally
(c) quite often

9 Have you ever lied about your background, your parentage or your wealth?

(a) never
(b) occasionally
(c) often

10 Are most of your friends:

(a) poorer than you are?
(b) about as well off as you are?
(c) richer than you are?

Check your Score!

Openness

1	(a) 1	(b) 2	(c) 3
2	(a) 3	(b) 2	(c) 1
3	(a) 3	(b) 1	
4	(a) 3	(b) 1	(c) 2
5	(a) 1	(b) 2	(c) 3
6	(a) 1	(b) 3	(c) 2
7	(a) 3	(b) 2	(c) 1
8	(a) 3	(b) 1	(c) 2
9	(a) 3	(b) 1	
10	(a) 3	(b) 1	

If you scored 20 or more, you are very outgoing — quite an extrovert.

Optimism

1	(a) 3	(b) 1	
2	(a) 2	(b) 3	(c) 1
3	(a) 3	(b) 1	(c) 2
4	(a) 3	(b) 1	(c) 2
5	(a) 3	(b) 1	(c) 2
6	(a) 3	(b) 2	(c) 1
7	(a) 3	(b) 2	(c) 1
8	(a) 3	(b) 2	(c) 1
9	(a) 1	(b) 2	(c) 3
10	(a) 1	(b) 3	(c) 2

If you scored 20 or more, optimism is a major driving force in your life.

Fear

1	(a) 2	(b) 3	(c) 1
2	(a) 3	(b) 1	(c) 2
3	(a) 3	(b) 1	(c) 1
4	(a) 1	(b) 2	(c) 3
5	(a) 1	(b) 3	(c) 2
6	(a) 1	(b) 2	(c) 3
7	(a) 1	(b) 3	(c) 3
8	(a) 1	(b) 3	(c) 1
9	(a) 3	(b) 1	(c) 2
10	(a) 1	(b) 2	(c) 3

If you scored 20 or more, fear is a major driving force in your life.

Obsessiveness

1	(a) 3	(b) 2	(c) 1
2	(a) 3	(b) 2	(c) 1
3	(a) 3	(b) 1	
4	(a) 3	(b) 1	
5	(a) 3	(b) 2	(c) 1
6	(a) 3	(b) 2	(c) 1
7	(a) 1	(b) 3	(c) 2
8	(a) 3	(b) 2	(c) 1
9	(a) 3	(b) 1	
10	(a) 3	(b) 1	

If you scored 20 or more, you are rather obsessional.

Vanity

1 (a) 3 (b) 1
2 (a) 1 (b) 3 (c) 3
3 (a) 3 (b) 1 (c) 2
4 (a) 2 (b) 3 (c) 1
5 (a) 1 (b) 2 (c) 3
6 (a) 1 (b) 3 (c) 3
7 (a) 3 (b) 2 (c) 1
8 (a) 3 (b) 2 (c) 1
9 (a) 3 (b) 1
10 (a) 1 (b) 2 (c) 3

If you scored 20 or more, vanity is a major driving force in your life.

Romanticism

1 (a) 3 (b) 1
2 (a) 1 (b) 3
3 (a) 3 (b) 1
4 (a) 3 (b) 1
5 (a) 3 (b) 1
6 (a) 3 (b) 1
7 (a) 3 (b) 1
8 (a) 3 (b) 1
9 (a) 3 (b) 1
10 (a) 1 (b) 3

If you scored 20 or more, you are very romantic.

Aggression

1 (a) 3 (b) 2 (c) 1
2 (a) 3 (b) 1 (c) 2
3 (a) 2 (b) 3 (c) 1
4 (a) 1 (b) 1 (c) 3
5 (a) 1 (b) 2 (c) 3
6 (a) 1 (b) 2 (c) 3
7 (a) 1 (b) 2 (c) 3
8 (a) 1 (b) 2 (c) 3
9 (a) 1 (b) 2 (c) 3
10 (a) 3 (b) 2 (c) 1

If you scored 20 or more, aggression is a major driving force in your life.

Lust

1 (a) 2 (b) 1 (c) 3
2 (a) 1 (b) 3
3 (a) 1 (b) 2 (c) 3
4 (a) 3 (b) 2 (c) 1
5 (a) 2 (b) 3 (c) 1
6 (a) 3 (b) 2 (c) 1
7 (a) 3 (b) 2 (c) 1
8 (a) 1 (b) 1 (c) 3
9 (a) 1 (b) 2 (c) 3
10 (a) 1 (b) 2 (c) 3

If you scored 20 or more, lust is a major driving force in your life.

Ambition

1 (a) 2 (b) 1 (c) 3
2 (a) 1 (b) 3 (c) 2
3 (a) 3 (b) 1 (c) 1
4 (a) 2 (b) 1 (c) 3
5 (a) 3 (b) 1
6 (a) 2 (b) 1 (c) 3
7 (a) 1 (b) 3 (c) 2
8 (a) 3 (b) 1 (c) 2
9 (a) 1 (b) 3
10 (a) 1 (b) 3 (c) 2

If you scored 20 or more, ambition is a major driving force in your life.

Snobbishness

1 (a) 3 (b) 1
2 (a) 1 (b) 2 (c) 3
3 (a) 3 (b) 2 (c) 1
4 (a) 3 (b) 2 (c) 1
5 (a) 1 (b) 2 (c) 3
6 (a) 3 (b) 2 (c) 1
7 (a) 1 (b) 2 (c) 3
8 (a) 1 (b) 2 (c) 3
9 (a) 1 (b) 2 (c) 3
10 (a) 1 (b) 2 (c) 3

If you scored 20 or more, you are rather a snob and your snobbishness affects your life.

How Many People Are You?

Eve had three faces. Ohio State University rapist 'Milligan' had ten separate people living inside his body. When psychiatrists interviewed 'Sybil', they found that she had 16 quite separate personalities, and at the Daytona Beach Human Resources Center, a patient called 'Eric' was found to have no less than 27 individual personalities. Altogether, psychiatrists and psychologists have reported over 200 cases of individual patients having distinct and conflicting personalities sharing these bodies.

Is the multiple personality all that unusual? I believe that we all have many different personalities. We are all many different people and our personalities change according to circumstances, our surroundings and, most important of all, the people we are with.

For example, you may think of your best friend, Jane, as being shy and sensitive. But is she always like that? With some people she may be demanding, even aggressive. To others she may seem saucy and sexy. And what about you? How many people are YOU? Only when you know the answer to that question, will you really understand yourself.

The truth is that all of us behave in different ways with different people. Our attitudes do not stay constant. We act differently with our employers, employees, spouses, neighbours, children, parents, doctors and friends. A young business executive may feel bitter towards his immediate boss. He may be sycophantic towards the chairman of the company he works for, lustful towards his young, shapely, blonde secretary and respectful towards his parents. He may be a tyrant to his children and his wife and a trusting and generous companion to his closest male friends. His chairman may despise him, his children may be afraid of him, his secretary may love him and his wife may loathe him.

However stable we may think we are, we will always seem different to different people. Your bank manager does not see the same 'you' that your tennis partners see. The local garage where you have had a row may dread your coming in. The local hairdressing salon, where you always tip heavily, may welcome you enthusiastically. We are none of us single individuals. If our parents described our virtues, our enemies would not recognize us. If our children described us, the chances are that our employers would not know who they were talking about.

The ten quizzes that follow are specially designed to help you find out how you respond in different circumstances. You can find out who you are at home, who you are at work, who you are with your best friend, who you are in bed, who you are at the doctor's and so on. Simply answer yes or no to each of the questions – and you will find out how many people you are and how you appear to the people you live and work with.

When you have completed each of the quizzes, take a look at the overall picture. Try to compare your different personalities. Do you behave differently at the doctor's from the way you behave while out shopping? Are you kind and thoughful with your best friend but aggressive and demanding with your partner? These quizzes will help you find out a lot about yourself. Life may never be the same again!

In *The Three Faces of Eve*, Joanne Woodward gave a powerful performance as a woman embodying three very different personalities, each fighting for supremacy.

*W*ho *A*re *Y*ou at the *S*hops?

1 You are in a clothes shop. The assistant has spent an hour showing you jackets, but you have not found anything you like. Would you leave without buying anything?

   yes

2 If you are buying apples do you usually insist on choosing the fruit yourself?

   yes

3 You are buying a sweater and you find that it has a mark on it. Would you ask for a reduction in the price?

   yes

4 Do you always take a shopping list with you — and stick to it?

   yes

5 Do you think shop assistants tend to be too pushy?

   yes

6 Do you always shop around and think carefully before buying major items?

   yes

7 You buy a radio. After six months it breaks down. Would you insist on a replacement?

   yes

8 You buy a piece of meat. When you get it home you find it is tough and inedible. Would you insist on either a refund or a free piece of meat?

   yes

9 After a visit to the supermarket you discover that you have been charged too much. Would you insist on a refund?

   yes

10 Do you get upset if shop assistants chatter and keep you waiting?

   yes

If you answered **Yes** 1-3 times, you are timid and you do not like making a fuss. To the shop assistant you are a mug.

If you answered **Yes** 4-7 times, you are usually polite but, if pushed, you will stand up for your rights.

If you answered **Yes** 8-10 times, you are a fighter and you stick up for yourself in shops.

Who Are You at the Doctors?

1 If your doctor kept you waiting for an hour, would you want to know why?

   yes

2 If you were told that you needed surgery, would you expect to be told exactly why?

   yes

3 If you were unsatisfied by your doctor, would you ask for a second opinion?

   yes

4 Would you protest if the receptionist told you that you could not have an appointment for a week?

   yes

5 Would you have the courage to write down things your doctor told you in his consulting room?

   yes

6 If your doctor asked you to take part in a clinical trial of a new drug, would you ask for more details before agreeing?

   yes

7 If you were still unhappy about the trial, would you refuse to take part?

   yes

8 Would you consider making a complaint if you thought your doctor had not treated you reasonably?

   yes

9 Do you feel patients have a right to know what is wrong with them?

   yes

10 Do you think doctors have rather an easy life?

   yes

If you answered **Yes** 1-3 times, you are probably shy and frightened when you see your doctor, and it shows.

If you answered **Yes** 4-7 times, you treat your doctor with respect but you have got sufficient concern for your health to make sure that you get well looked after.

If you answered **Yes** 8-10 times, your doctor probably quakes when he sees you coming. You treat him in the same way that you would treat anyone else providing a service.

Who Are You at Work?

1 There is a strike on, but you do not agree with it. Would you carry on working?

   yes

2 A friend of yours is dismissed unfairly. Would you intervene?

   yes

3 If you were refused permission to take a day off, would you take a day off anyway — and face the consequences later?

   yes

4 Would you ever resign on a matter of principle?

   yes

5 Would you protest if you felt that you were being treated unfairly?

   yes

6 Are you ever irritable with people you work with?

   yes

7 If you felt that your working conditions were unacceptable, would you complain?

   yes

8 You find that your company is doing something dishonest. Would you make an official complaint?

   yes

9 Your boss asks you to work over the weekend. Would you discuss money before agreeing?

   yes

10 If you could think of a better way of doing something, would you tell your boss?

   yes

If you answered **Yes** 1-3 times, you are a bit of a mouse.

If you answered **Yes** 4-7 times, you do not let people walk all over you, but you are sensible enough to avoid sticking your neck out too far. You are a realist at work.

If you scored **Yes** 8-10 times, you are confident and aggressive, and you are probably considered a leader by those you work with.

Who Are You on Holiday?

1 Do you think holidays cost too much?

yes

2 Do you think parents should try to keep young children quiet on beaches and in swimming pools etc?

yes

3 Do you think holidays are over-rated?

yes

4 Would you demand your money back if your holiday was a disaster?

yes

5 You are on the beach. Someone nearby has a radio turned up very loud. Would you complain?

yes

6 Do you always like to learn something or see something interesting when you are on holiday?

yes

7 If you go into an amusement arcade, do you decide in advance how much you will spend?

yes

8 Do you think holidaymakers tend to get a raw deal from holiday companies?

yes

9 Do you object to paying inflated prices for ice creams and soft drinks when you are on holiday?

yes

10 When you meet new friends on holiday, do you boast a little because you know that you will probably never see them again?

yes

If you answered **Yes** 1-3 times, you are easy-going and determined to enjoy yourself, regardless of the expense.

If you answered **Yes** 4-7 times, you try to enjoy yourself but well-established, natural habits are difficult to break. You do not like being ripped off.

If you answered **Yes** 8-10 times, you probably do not enjoy holidays very much. You spend most of the time worrying and complaining.

Who Are You with Your Parents?

1 Do they usually decide how you will spend your Christmas?

   yes

2 Do they usually decide where you will go on your holidays?

   yes

3 Do they ever interfere with your choice of friends?

   yes

4 Do you usually ask their advice before taking important decisions?

   yes

5 Do you feel afraid to contradict them?

   yes

6 Would you consult them before making a decision about your career?

   yes

7 Do you feel bad if you do not visit them regularly?

   yes

8 Do you feel bad if you do not telephone or write regularly?

   yes

9 Do you often feel that you have been a disappointment to them?

   yes

10 Would you talk to your parents before moving home?

   yes

If you answered **Yes** 1-3 times, you are independent and although you may love and respect your parents you do not let them run your life.

If you answered **Yes** 4-7 times, you are breaking away – but the apron strings still are not completely untied.

If you answered **Yes** 8-10 times, your parents probably still think of you as a small child. To them you may well appear immature and in need of support. In some ways, they are probably right.

Who Are You in a Car?

1 You are stuck behind someone on a fast road. Would you overtake on the wrong side?

   yes

2 Do you get very frustrated when you are stuck behind slow drivers?

   yes

3 If you had a minor motoring bump would you blame the other driver out of habit?

   yes

4 Do other drivers honk their horns a lot when you are driving?

   yes

5 Do you honk your horn a lot when you are driving?

   yes

6 Do you enjoy racing other drivers?

   yes

7 If another driver cut you up, would you chase him?

   yes

8 You are trying to park. You see someone struggling to get into a space. If you could get in first, would you steal the space?

   yes

9 Do you hate learner drivers?

   yes

10 You are in a traffic queue and you see a lone motorist trying to edge out of a side road. Would you keep very close to the car in front?

   yes

If you answered **Yes** 1-3 times, you seem a careful, cautious and thoughtful driver.

If you answered **Yes** 4-7 times, you try to be a good driver – but once you get behind a steering wheel you tend to become aggressive.

If you answered **Yes** 8-10 times, you remind me of Toad of Toad Hall: 'Toot, toot! Get off the roads, I'm coming. Get out of my way.' You are a road toad!

Who Are You With Your Best Friend?

1 Would you lend him/her money?

   yes

2 Would you lend him/her money without your partner knowing about it?

   yes

3 Would you lend him/her money, even if your partner disapproved?

   yes

4 Do you ever discuss your sex life with your best friend?

   yes

8 Your best friend is giving an important dinner party. He/she needs a waiter but cannot afford one. Would you dress up and take the job seriously?

   yes

9 Would you be prepared to lend your best friend any of your clothes?

   yes

10 Your best friend rings at three o'clock in the morning to tell you that he/she is stuck at the local railway station. Would you go out and fetch him/her? Or would you find someone who would?

   yes

5 Do you sometimes discuss money with your best friend?

   yes

6 If your best friend asked you to provide him/her with a false alibi for his/her spouse, would you oblige?

   yes

7 If your best friend asked you to provide him/her with a false alibi for the police would you oblige?

   yes

If you answered **Yes** 1-3 times, you do not take friendship too seriously.

If you answered **Yes** 4-7 times, you balance your friendship with good sense and responsibility to your family.

If you answered **Yes** 8-10 times, you are an excellent friend – thoughtful and, if anything, over-generous.

Who Are You in Bed?

1 Do you usually make the first move in bed?

   yes

2 Do you discuss your sex life with your friends?

   yes

3 Do you think you are a better-than-average lover?

   yes

4 Would you be prepared to try anything in (or out of) bed?

   yes

5 Do you ever use artificial aids, such as vibrators or sexy clothes?

   yes

6 Do you like trying new positions?

   yes

7 You are staying with friends. The bed creaks. Would you still make love?

   yes

8 Would you make love in a public place?

   yes

9 You are making love in the daytime and you suddenly realize that the window cleaner is watching. Would you carry on?

   yes

10 Would you take part in an orgy?

   yes

If you answered **Yes** 1-3 times, you are a fairly shy and uncertain lover.

If you answered **Yes** 4-7 times, you enjoy sex – but you have strict limits.

If you answered **Yes** 8-10 times, you are sexy and you know it. Sex is very important to you and you have few inhibitions.

*W*ho *A*re *Y*ou with *Y*our *C*hildren?

1   Do you think parents are entitled to respect from their children?

    yes

2   Do you think children have things too easy these days?

    yes

3   Do you have difficulty in talking to your children about important things?

    yes

4   Do you believe in punishing children if they behave badly?

    yes

5   Do you think that children should earn their pocket money?

    yes

6   Do you think that parents have the right to choose their children's friends?

    yes

7   Do you think it is a parent's job to push children to do well at school?

    yes

8   Do you think that parents should make sure that their children always look smart?

    yes

9   Do you believe in the saying, 'Children should be seen but not heard'?

    yes

10 Do you think parents should be very strict about things like bedtimes?

    yes

If you answered **Yes** 1-3 times, you are a softy and children know you are a softy.

If you answered **Yes** 4-7 times, you can be strict but the strictness is tempered with a good deal of love, kindness, affection and patience.

If you answered **Yes** 8-10 times, you probably do not get on too well with children. You are rather authoritarian.

Who Are You with Your Partner?

Would you say 'yes' without bothering to talk it over with your partner?

yes

8 When you are buying things for the home, do you make most of the major decisions?

yes

9 If you are both invited to a dinner party would you accept without talking it over?

yes

10 Do you win all or most of the arguments you and your partner have?

yes

1 Do you decide where you will both go for your holidays?

yes

2 You know your partner has done something illegal. Would you tell the police without waiting for an explanation?

yes

3 If you partner cried on your shoulder in public would you be embarrassed?

yes

4 Do you think your partner needs pushing a little if he/she is to get on?

yes

5 Do you alone make all or most of the important decisions about money?

yes

6 Do you usually wait for your partner to make a move after you have had an argument?

yes

7 You live with your partner. A relative asks if he/she can come to stay for a month.

If you answered **Yes** 1-3 times, you are the perfect partner. You are kind, thoughtful and considerate.

If you answered **Yes** 4-7 times, you are part of a solid, give-and-take relationship.

If you answered **Yes** 8-10 times, you are aggressive, demanding and selfish. It must be like living with Attila the Hun.

*U*nderstanding *R*elationships

Now that you have learned a little about yourself, you should try to learn how to assess your relationships with other people. After all, they have an enormous influence on your life in general and on your health in particular. It is in your relationships with others that the varying aspects of your personality most obviously come into play, with inevitable consequences. When your relationships with people who are close to you, or people with whom you work, go wrong then you will find yourself under a great deal of stress. Misunderstandings, often caused by misconceptions, can lead to disagreements and arguments which in their turn cause an enormous amount of physical and mental distress not only

1 Do you like him/her?

2 Do you love him/her?

3 Do you think he/she likes you?

4 Do you think he/she loves you?

5 Do you have sexual feelings about him/her?

6 Do you think he/she has sexual feelings about you?

7 What do you give most to the relationship?

8 What do you get most out of the relationship?

9 What does he/she give most to the relationship?

10 What does he/she get most out of the relationship?

11 Who is the stronger partner in the relationship?

12 Do you tend to lean on him/her a great deal?

13 Does he/she tend to lean on you a great deal?

14 Do you take him/her for granted?

15 Does he/she take you for granted?

16 Can he/she always rely on you for help?

17 Can you always rely on him/her for help?

18 Does he/she ever frighten you?

19 Do you think that you ever frighten him/her?

20 Are you dependent on him/her for money?

21 Is he/she dependent on you for money?

22 Would you trust him/her with money?

23 Do you think he/she would trust you with money?

to you, but to the people you share your life with.

If you are going to improve your relationship with others and reduce the risk of unnecessary confrontations developing it follows that you must make a real effort to learn as much as you can about your attitude to other people and their attitudes to you. Once you have discovered what your expectations of other people are (and what other people's expectations of you are) then you will be far less likely to have to face sudden and unexpected frustration or disappointment.

To make an assessment of your important relationships with others, draw up a list of all the people who are close to you in any way. Include friends and relatives as well as neighbours and people with whom you work. Next, go through the following list of questions for each individual on your list. The answers you produce will help you understand your relationships with others a little better.

24 Would you trust him/her with your life?

25 Do you think he/she would trust you with his/her life?

26 Do you always talk kindly about him/her when he/she is not present?

27 Do you think he/she always talks kindly about you when you are not present?

28 What are his/her greatest ambitions?

29 What are his/her greatest loves?

30 What are his/her greatest fears?

31 What are his/her greatest strengths?

32 What are his/her greatest weaknesses?

33 What do you think is the most important thing in his/her life?

34 Do you benefit financially from the relationship?

35 Does he/she benefit financially from the relationship?

36 What annoys you most about him/her?

37 What do you think annoys him/her most about you?

38 If your car broke down at three o'clock in the morning could you ring him/her for help?

39 If his/her car broke down at three o'clock in the morning do you think he/she would feel able to ring you for help?

40 If you telephoned for help do you think he/she would help you?

41 If he/she telephoned for help would you help?

42 Do you trust him/her?

43 Do you think he/she trusts you?

Finally, here are some basic guidelines that will help you create new and reliable friendships.

When you meet a new friend, do not allow past prejudices and experiences to have too much influence on the relationship. If you have previously had an unfortunate experience with a bald man with a beard, you may automatically dislike anyone who has a bald head and a beard. But not all bald, bearded men are bad! If you judge people by the way they dress, you will only ever make friends with people who have a social or cultural background similar to yours.

What does he think about redheads? . . . How does she react to men with no hair at all? . . . Social constraints may force us to be outwardly amiable when we first meet people, whilst inwardly we bring to bear past influences on our impressions of new acquaintances. These prejudices cloud our picture of who that person really is.

Remember that other people have feelings, fears, ambitions, loves and hates which vary considerably from your own. Consequently, their attitudes towards specific events may also vary considerably from yours. If you always expect other people to respond in the same way as you, you will end up constantly being disappointed. Try to learn as much as you can about other people; try to answer the preceding questionnaire whenever you make new friends. The more you know about the people around you, the stronger your relationships will be.

Do not allow other people's prejudices to influence your attitudes to people you hardly know. Remember that any relationship is a result of an interaction between two people with quite separate sets of needs and ambitions. If you accept other people's judgements, you are accepting their needs and ambitions.

2
Control Your
estructive Emotions

Confusion and delusion are depicted in Bosch's fifteenth-century version of *The Garden of Earthly Delights* into which humanity was cast after the fall of man. In this nightmarish fantasy, the seven deadly sins thrive like weeds. In our lives our emotional responses to situations are sometimes negative and therefore destructive. We need to learn how to recognize and deal with destructive emotions in a positive and constructive way.

The quizzes in the last chapter should have helped you learn a little about yourself and how your personality affects, and is affected by, the world around you. Now that you know yourself better, you should be able to spot your weak points and learn to recognize the sorts of circumstances which are most likely to damage your health. Most important of all, you should have discovered enough about yourself to understand some of your relationships with others.

When trying to understand your relationships with other people you should never forget that we all automatically adapt our attitudes and our actions to suit the people we are with – and to suit our expectations of how they will behave and how they will expect us to behave! We act differently with our lovers, spouses, employers, neighbours, doctors, friends, competitors and relatives. When you go into your doctor's surgery, for example, your relationship with your doctor – and your understanding of that relationship – will influence the way you speak and the way you behave. You may be frightened but you may feel uncomfortable about sharing your fears. You may be angry but you may feel shy about letting your doctor know that you are angry. Undoubtedly you will put a different emphasis on things when talking to him or her than you use when talking to a close friend or relative. If you have thought about the way he or she will respond then you may adapt your behaviour to suit your expected response: if you think you will be treated without respect or patience you may walk into your doctor's consulting room and shout at him or her before he or she has begun to speak! Your imagination will control what happens.

In this chapter, I want to concentrate on five quite specific emotional responses – each one of which is perfectly natural, but each one of which can also damage your health in a very significant way. First, I will help you find out just how vulnerable you are to each one of these negative forces. Then I will show you how you can deal with these natural, inevitable forces in a positive and constructive way. The five destructive emotions which you must learn to overcome are boredom, guilt, hypochondriasis, sadness and anger.

*B*oredom

Mention the word 'stress' to most people and they think of executives rushing around from one meeting to another, or of taxi drivers struggling to find a way through busy city traffic. However, inactivity and boredom can cause just as much stress as having too much to do and being under too much pressure.

There are, I believe, four groups of people whose lives are threatened by boredom.

First, there are the many millions who have retired too soon and who have too little to do in their later years. These days, many people retire, in perfect health, at 60, 55 or even 50, and then discover that life without work can too easily become dull, purposeless and boring. To the man or woman who has spent his or her life working,

early retirement can result in a sense of worthlessness.

Second, boredom is, without a doubt, a major cause of stress among many women who are tied to the home because of their responsibilities to their children and husbands. Hunting for lost socks and ironing shirts is not work which many women find demanding or satisfying – particularly when their labours are too often unappreciated.

Third, boredom is common among the many people whose daily work is undemanding and unrewarding. There are millions of men and women who spend their days acting as nursemaids to huge, complex pieces of machinery. Machines have become so

*H*ow *t*o *D*eal *w*ith *B*oredom *i*n *a* *H*ealthy *w*ay

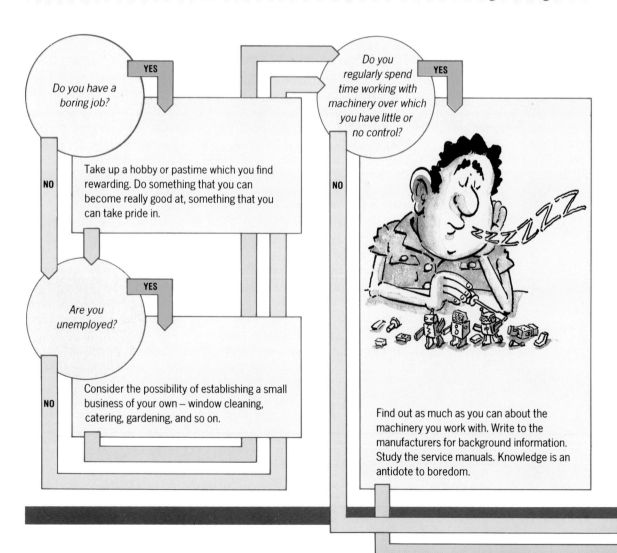

Do you have a boring job?

YES — Take up a hobby or pastime which you find rewarding. Do something that you can become really good at, something that you can take pride in.

NO

Are you unemployed?

YES — Consider the possibility of establishing a small business of your own – window cleaning, catering, gardening, and so on.

NO

Do you regularly spend time working with machinery over which you have little or no control?

YES

NO

Find out as much as you can about the machinery you work with. Write to the manufacturers for background information. Study the service manuals. Knowledge is an antidote to boredom.

sophisticated that they are too often regarded as the principal force in any working relationship. The individual worker is left with little chance to express his own personality or to feel any sense of pride in what he does.

Finally, boredom is common among the many millions who are unemployed. There have been a number of reports published which have shown that unemployment is a major cause of stress-induced disease. People who are unemployed – and who are not sure how to spend their days – have a higher-than-average risk of developing stomach ulcers, heart disease, asthma and skin problems, such as eczema.

If great chunks of your life are unspeakably dull and if boredom is a major cause of stress, do not despair. There are ways in which you can add zest to your life.

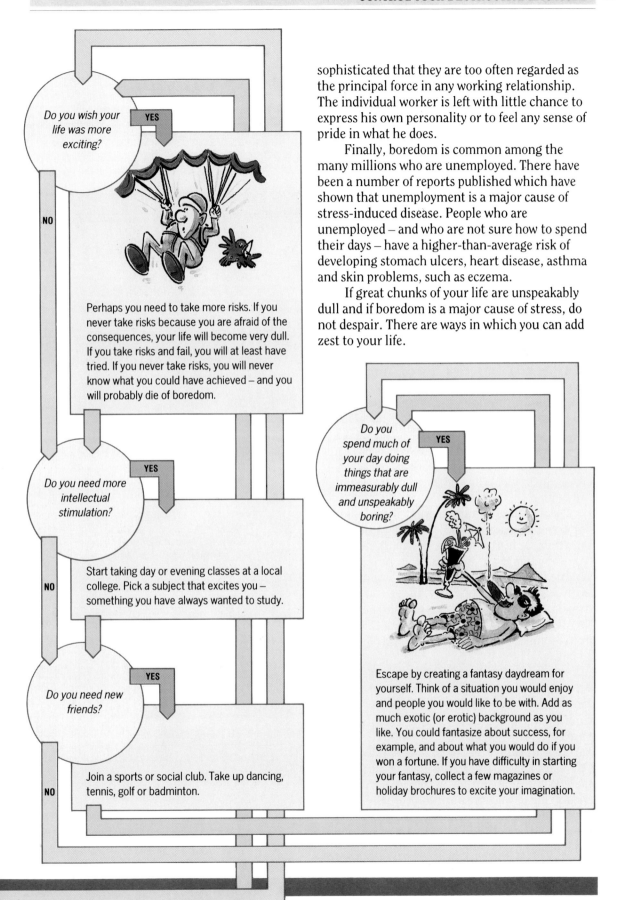

Do you wish your life was more exciting? **YES**

Perhaps you need to take more risks. If you never take risks because you are afraid of the consequences, your life will become very dull. If you take risks and fail, you will at least have tried. If you never take risks, you will never know what you could have achieved – and you will probably die of boredom.

Do you need more intellectual stimulation? **YES**

Start taking day or evening classes at a local college. Pick a subject that excites you – something you have always wanted to study.

Do you need new friends? **YES**

Join a sports or social club. Take up dancing, tennis, golf or badminton.

Do you spend much of your day doing things that are immeasurably dull and unspeakably boring? **YES**

Escape by creating a fantasy daydream for yourself. Think of a situation you would enjoy and people you would like to be with. Add as much exotic (or erotic) background as you like. You could fantasize about success, for example, and about what you would do if you won a fortune. If you have difficulty in starting your fantasy, collect a few magazines or holiday brochures to excite your imagination.

Guilt

Guilt is one of the most damaging of human emotions, yet is usually built on love. Difficult to define in practical terms, it is hard to distinguish from what most of us call conscience. We feel guilty when we have done wrong or when we have failed to do something that we know we should have done. We then torture ourselves with recriminations.

Most guilt falls into one of two categories. First, there is the guilt that results from personal relationships. Sometimes, guilt is produced deliberately, as when a parent says to a son or daughter, 'You wouldn't do that if you loved me'. The sibling, who has almost certainly already done 'that' (whatever it is) then feels guilty because he does not love his parent. Sometimes, guilt is produced more subtly, if, for example, a mother says to her daughter, 'Don't worry about me, you go off and enjoy yourself. I'll be all right'. When the daughter goes off, she *does* worry and feels guilty for abandoning her mother.

Second is the guilt which results from the teachings of those around us. By the time we leave childhood, most of us have a well-established inbuilt sense of right and wrong. This is not inherited, but comes from social and religious codes which have been set by example and instruction.

Some of these acquired principles are sound. For example, most of us feel guilty if we steal something or hurt someone; we have been taught that these things are antisocial. Yet some of our acquired fears are not so logical. For example, many people feel guilty if they enjoy themselves, if they have sex, if they earn too much money or if they lie in bed on a Sunday. Such guilt is learned from teachers, politicians, parents and pundits of all kinds.

All this guilt creates a feeling of inadequacy. We feel guilty when we fail to live up to the expectations of others. As a result, we lose confidence, and this is why guilt causes so much physical and mental damage. Because we regard ourselves as failures, we push ourselves too hard.

Guilt is particularly damaging because it is there all the time, turning us into workaholics and forcing us to strive until we drop. Guilt is a major cause of heart disease, stomach ulceration, asthma, skin conditions and a hundred and one other problems.

How to Deal with Guilt in a Healthy way

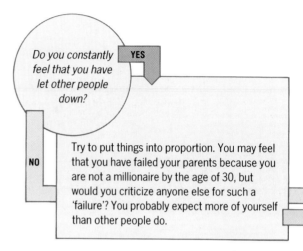

Do you constantly feel that you have let other people down?

YES / **NO**

Try to put things into proportion. You may feel that you have failed your parents because you are not a millionaire by the age of 30, but would you criticize anyone else for such a 'failure'? You probably expect more of yourself than other people do.

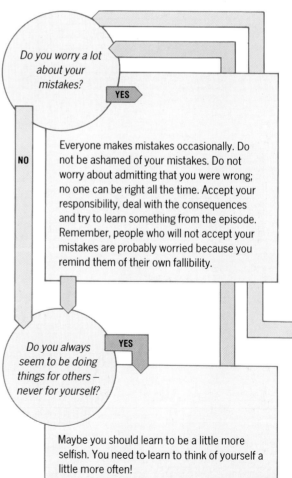

Do you worry a lot about your mistakes?

YES / **NO**

Everyone makes mistakes occasionally. Do not be ashamed of your mistakes. Do not worry about admitting that you were wrong; no one can be right all the time. Accept your responsibility, deal with the consequences and try to learn something from the episode. Remember, people who will not accept your mistakes are probably worried because you remind them of their own fallibility.

Do you always seem to be doing things for others – never for yourself?

YES

Maybe you should learn to be a little more selfish. You need to learn to think of yourself a little more often!

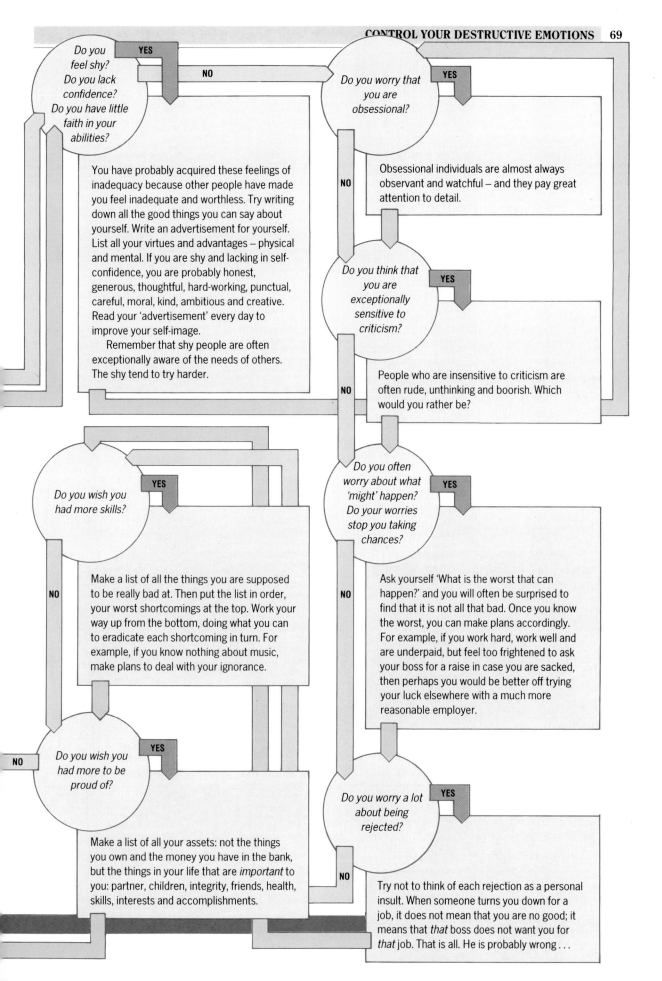

Do you feel shy? Do you lack confidence? Do you have little faith in your abilities?

YES / NO

You have probably acquired these feelings of inadequacy because other people have made you feel inadequate and worthless. Try writing down all the good things you can say about yourself. Write an advertisement for yourself. List all your virtues and advantages – physical and mental. If you are shy and lacking in self-confidence, you are probably honest, generous, thoughtful, hard-working, punctual, careful, moral, kind, ambitious and creative. Read your 'advertisement' every day to improve your self-image.

Remember that shy people are often exceptionally aware of the needs of others. The shy tend to try harder.

Do you worry that you are obsessional?

YES / NO

Obsessional individuals are almost always observant and watchful – and they pay great attention to detail.

Do you think that you are exceptionally sensitive to criticism?

YES / NO

People who are insensitive to criticism are often rude, unthinking and boorish. Which would you rather be?

Do you wish you had more skills?

YES / NO

Make a list of all the things you are supposed to be really bad at. Then put the list in order, your worst shortcomings at the top. Work your way up from the bottom, doing what you can to eradicate each shortcoming in turn. For example, if you know nothing about music, make plans to deal with your ignorance.

Do you often worry about what 'might' happen? Do your worries stop you taking chances?

YES / NO

Ask yourself 'What is the worst that can happen?' and you will often be surprised to find that it is not all that bad. Once you know the worst, you can make plans accordingly. For example, if you work hard, work well and are underpaid, but feel too frightened to ask your boss for a raise in case you are sacked, then perhaps you would be better off trying your luck elsewhere with a much more reasonable employer.

Do you wish you had more to be proud of?

YES / NO

Make a list of all your assets: not the things you own and the money you have in the bank, but the things in your life that are *important* to you: partner, children, integrity, friends, health, skills, interests and accomplishments.

Do you worry a lot about being rejected?

YES / NO

Try not to think of each rejection as a personal insult. When someone turns you down for a job, it does not mean that you are no good; it means that *that* boss does not want you for *that* job. That is all. He is probably wrong . . .

*H*ypochondriasis

Most of us worry about our health. There is nothing unusual in that. Few of us enjoy pain or illness. We want to stay healthy and live for as long as possible. However, our natural anxiety about our health becomes a major, negative influence when we start using illness to help us cope with problems in our lives; when we allow symptoms to develop so that they provide us with an excuse for not doing things that we are frightened of or do not want to do.

Most of us occasionally use illness to avoid unpleasant tasks. Getting a cold can be a good way of avoiding a meeting you do not want to go to. Backache can provide a reasonable excuse for avoiding a sporting confrontation that you do not relish. A headache is the classic way to avoid unwanted sex. Simple physical symptoms can give us solid excuses (excuses that bring us sympathy) whenever we are frightened, embarrassed, ashamed or just plain nervous.

However, what starts as a useful excuse can sometimes become a way of life, and big problems can develop. Using the symptoms of ill-health in this way can, in the long run, produce many special difficulties. The basic fear will not have disappeared and an apparently real, physical condition may develop.

It is only too easy for us to teach ourselves – or others – to use sickness and fears of ill-health in such a way that our lives are dominated by illness. We can think ourselves into chronic illness by carelessly using symptoms to help us obtain short-term relief.

When a child discovers that he can avoid a spelling test at school by complaining of a tummy ache, he is learning to use ill-health to help him avoid an unpleasant experience. When his parents then give him extra love, sympathy and cuddles, let him stay in bed, put the television set in his room, give him comics and feed him ice cream and chocolate, they are teaching the child that the rewards of hypochondriasis are too great to be ignored. Many chronic invalids acquired their illnesses by avoiding minor inconveniences. The mind can easily learn to use the body – and the body's weaknesses – to avoid threats, confrontation and other real-life problems.

Over the years I have met many patients who have subconsciously used and exacerbated quite genuine physical problems to help them deal with social or personal crises. A young solicitor used his migraines to help him avoid meeting a particularly objectionable client. Until he was faced with the truth, his migraines were threatening his practice. A young woman used her menstrual problems to avoid intercourse with a husband she no longer loved, and an elderly lady used her mild arthritis (which then disabled her completely) in order to avoid travelling on holiday with her sister.

How to Deal with Hypochondriasis in a Healthy way

Do you suffer from any symptoms which disappear and reappear at apparently irregular and unexpected intervals?

Do you tend to retire to bed if you are worried, upset or anxious?

Do you have any long-term medical problem for which your doctor has been unable to find any explanation?

When you were ill as a child, did your mother make a tremendous fuss of you?

When you were young, did you ever use physical symptoms of any kind to enable you to stay away from school?

You could be using symptoms in order to protect yourself from unpleasant experiences. You must ask yourself what benefits you gain from the illness. Ask yourself what it is that you find so difficult to accept. For example, if your migraine headaches become particularly bad when you have to meet a particular person, ask yourself what it is about the meetings that frightens you. What is the worst that person can do to you? If you always get stomach ache on the first Thursday of the month, ask yourself what always worries you on or around that date. If your partner always gets a headache when you make sexual overtures, ask yourself what is wrong with the relationship – not what you can do about the headaches. When your mind is using your body, the solution to the body's problem can only be found by studying your mind.

Do you invariably develop mild physical symptoms (such as diarrhea, headaches, backache etc) when you are under pressure or stressed?

Do you enjoy being looked after when you are ill?

Do you regularly have to miss important but unpleasant appointments through ill-health?

Have you ever felt secretly pleased when you have developed an illness which has enabled you to avoid an unpleasant social event?

Has anyone ever accused you of malingering?

NO NO YES YES NO NO YES YES NO YES YES NO YES NO YES NO YES NO NO

*S*adness

Sadness is our natural way of reacting to problems, pressures and stresses that affect us in a deeply personal way – and the natural, human way of showing that we are sad is by crying. When we are young, if unhappy, we cry quite naturally to make it clear to our parents and those around us that we need attention and would like sympathy and love. As we grow older, we find that shedding tears is a quick way to tell the people who love us that we need love and affection.

Recently, scientists have even managed to show that shedding tears also provides us with a genuine, physical release. Tears shed for emotional reasons have a higher protein content than tears shed because of the wind or other physical irritations. Crying helps the body get rid of harmful physical wastes.

However, many people regard this obvious physical sign of distress as a sign of weakness and even emotional instability. Boys, in particular, are taught by society that it is wrong to cry and that they should bottle up their feelings, rather than allow themselves to be seen with tears on their cheeks. The truth is that, when people *don't* cry, they suffer very badly when under pressure. People who suppress tears, end up suppressing their emotions and storing their sadness inside themselves.

Damage is done in three separate ways. First, when tears are not allowed out, the unwanted chemical wastes are also retained. Second, by not crying we deny ourselves the much needed love and attention that would have helped us to cope. Third, the emotional release that most of us gain by crying is also lost. After crying, people usually feel calm and rested in a strange sort of way. Those who deny themselves the chance to cry, deny themselves a very powerful therapeutic aid.

Crying, it seems clear, is an excellent way of dealing with sadness. By allowing ourselves to cry, we can conquer a powerful and potentially destructive, negative emotion.

Crying is the natural, human way of showing unhappiness. It tells the people who love us that we need love and affection.

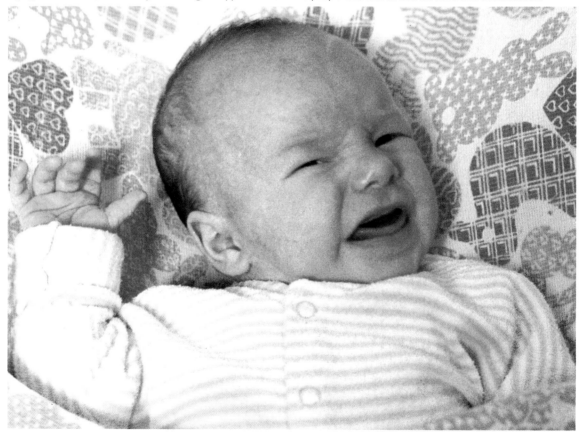

Do **Y**ou **D**eal with **S**adness in a **H**ealthy way?

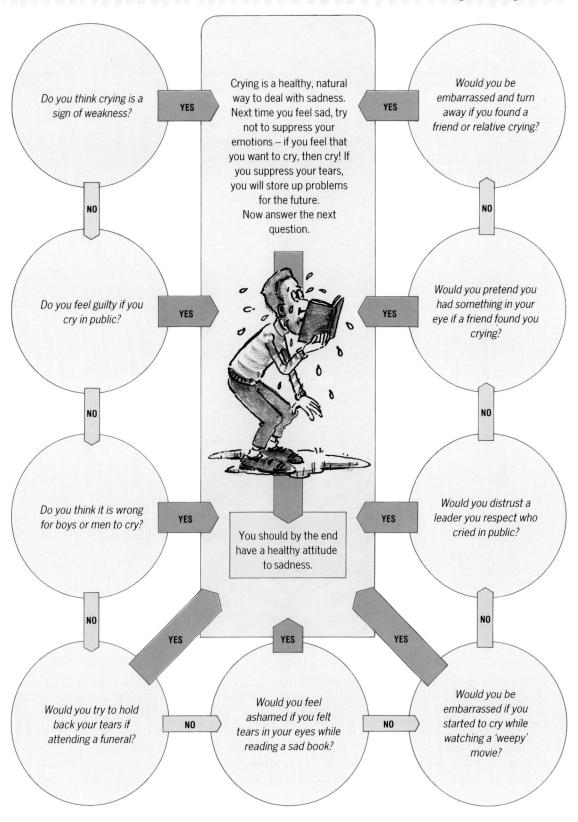

Do you think crying is a sign of weakness?

YES

Crying is a healthy, natural way to deal with sadness. Next time you feel sad, try not to suppress your emotions – if you feel that you want to cry, then cry! If you suppress your tears, you will store up problems for the future.
Now answer the next question.

YES

Would you be embarrassed and turn away if you found a friend or relative crying?

NO

Do you feel guilty if you cry in public?

YES

YES

Would you pretend you had something in your eye if a friend found you crying?

NO

Do you think it is wrong for boys or men to cry?

YES

You should by the end have a healthy attitude to sadness.

YES

Would you distrust a leader you respect who cried in public?

NO

NO

YES **YES** **YES** **NO**

Would you try to hold back your tears if attending a funeral?

NO

Would you feel ashamed if you felt tears in your eyes while reading a sad book?

NO

Would you be embarrassed if you started to cry while watching a 'weepy' movie?

*A*nger

Whatever causes it, anger – or rather the supression of it – can damage both your physical and mental health. Many diseases are caused by suppressing anger. High blood pressure, heart attacks and strokes are all common among those who do not allow themselves to express anger. Stored, unreleased anger can produce all the symptoms of stress-induced disease. The extra flow of acid into the stomach can help cause indigestion and, eventually, a gastric or duodenal ulcer may develop. Mental symptoms, such as insomnia, are also a common consequence. Anger is so often linked to pain that it is no coincidence that we frequently describe painful-looking wounds or burns as 'angry'.

However, anger does not only produce disease in this direct way. There is now evidence that people who refuse to allow themselves to show their anger are more likely to develop diseases such as cancer than individuals who respond to their anger in a more natural way. For example, a major study in London showed that women who suppress their anger are more prone to develop breast cancer than women who let their feelings show when they feel angry.

Anger is one of the most fundamental human feelings. It can be produced by frustration, by disappointment and by what we perceive as injustice. It is fired by aggression in others, by their indifference, impatience and thoughtlessness.

*H*ow to *D*eal with *A*nger in a *H*ealthy way

Do you ever get angry? YES

NO

Everyone gets angry from time to time. Anger is a perfectly natural and healthy response to some types of stress. Learn to recognize when you are heading for a confrontation and try not to push people into corners – leave them an escape route. When you feel yourself getting angry, decide if your anger is justified – is the problem *worth* getting angry about?

Do you suppress your anger? YES

NO

If you feel your anger is justified, then let it out. Complain if your complaint is justified. If you store your anger, it will build into frustration and damage your health.

Do you ever feel like hitting people? Does anger build up inside you? YES

Learn to get rid of your anger. Take part in some energetic physical activity. Hit a tennis ball, for example. Paint the face of someone you dislike on a punchball – and then try hitting the stuffing out of him. Try chopping wood, beating carpets or digging the garden, or take a pile of old plates into the garage and smash them. Getting rid of your aggressive feelings will leave you far healthier.

3

uild up your

ositive emotions

Do not limit yourself to only one day a year of comic relief! The beneficial effects of laughter – both mental and physical – can and do surpass medical aid. Bring laughter into your life and into the lives of those around you whenever you can. It is deservedly called 'the best medicine'.

Just as negative emotions can have a harmful effect on your mind and your body, so positive emotions can have a useful one. If you feel miserable or depressed, you will take longer to recover from an illness than if you feel cheerful and optimistic. If you surround yourself with people who are permanently gloomy and you face every problem and fresh challenge with pessimism in your heart, then your life will be an almost endless series of disappointments and missed opportunities.

Conversely, if you fill your life with joy, love, purpose and enthusiasm then you will be far less likely to suffer from any of the many common stress-induced physical or mental disorders – or any other physical or mental problem. Amazing though it sounds, there is now a growing amount of evidence to show that you can laugh yourself to good health, that love can heal many wounds and that by putting goals into your life you will stand a far better chance of staying healthy and defeating all kinds of illness.

In every relationship – and every aspect of each relationship — your behaviour will be influenced by all your primary driving forces and by all the driving forces which influence the other people involved. Although one particular emotion may appear to be dominant, other emotions will still be there, simmering away and affecting what happens.

For example, you may approach a meeting feeling happy and optimistic. You may firmly believe that everything will go well. However, although your positive emotions appear to be dominating, there will always be destructive emotions waiting in the wings. Your vanity may lead you to become over confident, your aggressiveness may make you too sure of yourself or you may become careless and make a mistake.

Just as important is the fact that the same emotional hazards that can affect you can affect the people you are with. Indeed, you should not forget that your success may inspire the rise of destructive emotions in others. Your happiness may lead to someone else's fear or your optimism may make someone else feel a failure.

Always try to imagine how other people think and respond. With a little thought you can help them build up their positive emotions, too; and, in the long run, their delight will benefit you as well.

*L*aughter

Laughter is more than just a pleasant experience or a momentary joy. It is a positive, natural phenomenon which can help ensure that your body stays healthy. When you laugh, your lungs are exercised and your heart is given excellent 'tuning up' exercises. More importantly, special healing hormones are released inside your body! After a good laugh, your blood pressure will be lower, your breathing will be easier and you will sleep better.

Even smiling can help! There is evidence that when you smile, your whole body becomes calmer. Try it: next time you are feeling miserable, try putting a really cheerful smile on your face. You will find it difficult to stay quite so sad. Try making your eyes sparkle with laughter and you will notice the effect even more.

The value of laughter and happiness is now so well established that there are medical experts who claim that doctors could often do more for the health of their patients by helping them to laugh and to smile than by giving them pills.

*D*o *Y*ou *N*eed more

Answer the following ten questions as carefully and as honestly as you can. Then check your score to find out if you need to put more laughter into your life.

1   How often do you have a really good laugh?

   (a)   at least once most days
   (b)   at least once every week
   (c)   at least once a month
   (d)   not very often

2   If someone plays a practical joke on you, do you:

   (a)   see the funny side straight away?
   (b)   usually see the funny side eventually?
   (c)   usually fail to see the funny side?

3   You are with a group of friends and someone tells an anecdote which makes you look foolish. Do you:

   (a)   probably feel offended and sulk or get cross?
   (b)   feel embarrassed but join in the laughter straight away?
   (c)   join in the general laughter without any embarrassment?
   (d)   react a bit stiffily at first but eventually smile a little?

4   You are making love. Your partner suddenly starts to giggle. Would you:

   (a)   be surprised, offended and deeply hurt?
   (b)   want to know what was so funny – and then probably start laughing?
   (c)   start laughing straight away – even if you did not know why?

Laughter in your Life?

5 How many books can you name that have made you laugh out loud?

(a) *none*
(b) *1 or 2*
(c) *3 or more*

6 How many films can you name that have made you laugh out loud?

(a) *none*
(b) *1 or 2*
(c) *3 or more*

7 How many TV programmes can you name that have made you laugh out loud?

(a) *none*
(b) *1 or 2*
(c) *3 or more*

8 How many stand-up comedians can you name who make you laugh?

(a) *none*
(b) *1 or 2*
(c) *3 or more*

9 You are at a party and a group of friends start to engage in harmless but silly antics. Would you:

(a) *join in straight away?*
(b) *maybe join in?*
(c) *watch?*
(d) *keep out of their way and leave as soon as possible?*
(e) *you do not have any friends who would behave like that*

10 A street entertainer has gathered a huge crowd – most of the people are laughing heartily. You are not in any hurry. Would you:

(a) *stop and enjoy the show?*
(b) *sneak a quick look but then carry on?*
(c) *hurry by without looking?*
(d) *hurry by and look for a policeman so that you can make a complaint about the noise?*

Check your Score!

1	(a) 4	(b) 3	(c) 2	(d) 1
2	(a) 3	(b) 2	(c) 1	
3	(a) 1	(b) 3	(c) 4	(d) 2
4	(a) 1	(b) 2	(c) 3	
5	(a) 1	(b) 2	(c) 3	
6	(a) 1	(b) 2	(c) 3	
7	(a) 1	(b) 2	(c) 3	
8	(a) 1	(b) 2	(c) 3	
9	(a) 5	(b) 4	(c) 3	(d) 2	(e) 1
10	(a) 4	(b) 3	(c) 2	(d) 1

If you scored 25-35

You laugh a lot and you are undoubtedly great fun to be with. You are almost certainly a real tonic to your friends – and to people who hardly know you.

If you scored 17-24

You have a fairly healthy attitude to life – but you tend to hold back sometimes. Perhaps you feel guilty about being seen having a good time in public. Perhaps you feel embarrassed if you laugh out loud. Perhaps you feel that your position, age or status mean that you should be restrained. Stop worrying! Let your hair down a little, follow your natural instincts and do not let your fears about what other people will think interfere with your desire – and ability – to enjoy yourself.

If you scored 16 or less

You really do need to loosen up and take yourself less seriously. You have, I suspect, a tendency to be a little pompous occasionally. If you would let more laughter and fun into your life and loosen up a little, then you would enjoy life more, make more friends, feel and be much healthier.

*H*ow to *P*ut more *L*aughter into your *L*ife

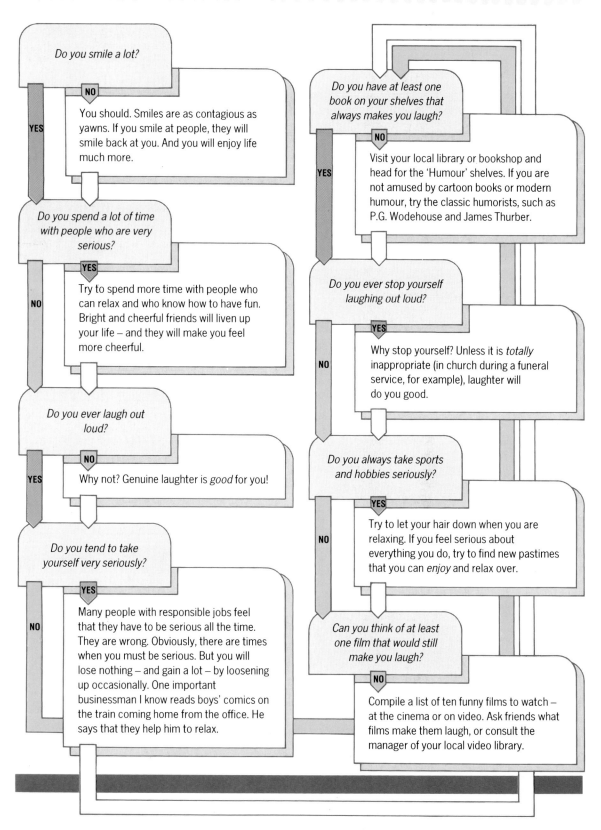

Do you smile a lot?

NO — You should. Smiles are as contagious as yawns. If you smile at people, they will smile back at you. And you will enjoy life much more.

YES ↓

Do you spend a lot of time with people who are very serious?

YES — Try to spend more time with people who can relax and who know how to have fun. Bright and cheerful friends will liven up your life – and they will make you feel more cheerful.

NO ↓

Do you ever laugh out loud?

NO — Why not? Genuine laughter is *good* for you!

YES ↓

Do you tend to take yourself very seriously?

YES — Many people with responsible jobs feel that they have to be serious all the time. They are wrong. Obviously, there are times when you must be serious. But you will lose nothing – and gain a lot – by loosening up occasionally. One important businessman I know reads boys' comics on the train coming home from the office. He says that they help him to relax.

NO ↓

Do you have at least one book on your shelves that always makes you laugh?

NO — Visit your local library or bookshop and head for the 'Humour' shelves. If you are not amused by cartoon books or modern humour, try the classic humorists, such as P.G. Wodehouse and James Thurber.

YES ↓

Do you ever stop yourself laughing out loud?

YES — Why stop yourself? Unless it is *totally* inappropriate (in church during a funeral service, for example), laughter will do you good.

NO ↓

Do you always take sports and hobbies seriously?

YES — Try to let your hair down when you are relaxing. If you feel serious about everything you do, try to find new pastimes that you can *enjoy* and relax over.

NO ↓

Can you think of at least one film that would still make you laugh?

NO — Compile a list of ten funny films to watch – at the cinema or on video. Ask friends what films make them laugh, or consult the manager of your local video library.

*O*ptimism

If you look at all your friends and relatives, you will probably find that very few of the people you know well are always optimistic or invariably pessimistic. Most people hold a mixture of both viewpoints. However, I suspect you will find that most of the people you meet tend to be largely optimistic or mainly pessimistic. I think you will also agree that people who are basically pessimistic tend to have unhappier (and less healthy) lives than people who are intrinsically optimistic.

If you get up in the morning thinking of all the terrible things you have got to do and of all the things that can go wrong, it will not take much to turn a potentially bad day into a horrendous one. If you are expecting trouble and awaiting problems, then each time something goes wrong, your gloom will deepen. Inevitably, the more you expect things to go wrong, the more they will. As you go through the day, so the people you meet will be depressed by your demeanour and your general sense of gloom and pessimism. By evening, your pessimism will have probably taken you into a dark depression. Confusion, fear and frustration will hourly make things worse.

To find out how much pessimism is affecting your life, go back to page 40 and check the personality quiz there. If you are naturally pessimistic, it will not be easy for you to convert yourself into a full-blooded optimist. It *will*, however, be possible for you to temper your pessimism with a greater degree of optimism; to dilute your natural sense of pessimism with a healthy splash of optimism.

*H*ow to become *M*ore *O*ptimistic

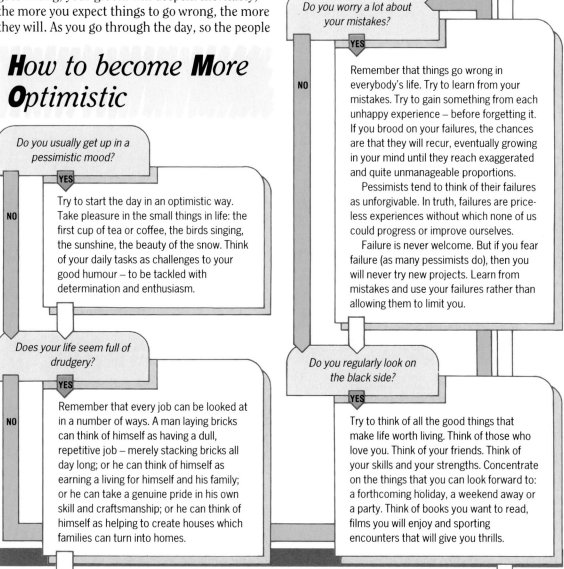

Do you usually get up in a pessimistic mood?

YES Try to start the day in an optimistic way. Take pleasure in the small things in life: the first cup of tea or coffee, the birds singing, the sunshine, the beauty of the snow. Think of your daily tasks as challenges to your good humour – to be tackled with determination and enthusiasm.

NO

Does your life seem full of drudgery?

YES Remember that every job can be looked at in a number of ways. A man laying bricks can think of himself as having a dull, repetitive job – merely stacking bricks all day long; or he can think of himself as earning a living for himself and his family; or he can take a genuine pride in his own skill and craftsmanship; or he can think of himself as helping to create houses which families can turn into homes.

NO

Do you worry a lot about your mistakes?

YES Remember that things go wrong in everybody's life. Try to learn from your mistakes. Try to gain something from each unhappy experience – before forgetting it. If you brood on your failures, the chances are that they will recur, eventually growing in your mind until they reach exaggerated and quite unmanageable proportions.

Pessimists tend to think of their failures as unforgivable. In truth, failures are price-less experiences without which none of us could progress or improve ourselves.

Failure is never welcome. But if you fear failure (as many pessimists do), then you will never try new projects. Learn from mistakes and use your failures rather than allowing them to limit you.

NO

Do you regularly look on the black side?

YES Try to think of all the good things that make life worth living. Think of those who love you. Think of your friends. Think of your skills and your strengths. Concentrate on the things that you can look forward to: a forthcoming holiday, a weekend away or a party. Think of books you want to read, films you will enjoy and sporting encounters that will give you thrills.

Love

She was in her early twenties, dark-haired, pale and stunningly attractive. He was a year or two older, short, slightly stocky and freckle-faced. I was a newly-qualified, junior hospital doctor. They had been married for about six months and she had been brought into the hospital suffering from meningitis. We had done everything we could, but the infection seemed to be winning. Just about every doctor in the hospital had been called in to advise and we did not know what else to do.

It looked as though she was going to die. He would not leave the hospital. The ward sister begged him to go home to rest, but he would not go. He sat by her bedside for hour after hour after hour. He held her hand, he stroked her cheek, he talked to her, he told her that he loved her, he wiped away his tears with her hand, he kissed her gently on the lips and he murmured her name over and over again. He would not let her go from him. Slowly he hauled her back from the gates of the unknown, eternal life. He paid off the ferryman and sent him back across the Styx with no passenger. Little by little, she regained her strength and her grasp on life.

The consultant physician who had been looking after her was puzzled. He could not explain her recovery; it defied all scientific sense. Doctors do not like recoveries which defy scientific sense. It reminds them of how little they know. The hospital chaplain, who had visited her twice a day, claimed a victory for his God. It was, he insisted, nothing short of a miracle.

I had no doubt at all about what had saved her. It was clear to me that she had been rescued by the power of love. It was the first time I had realized that even high-technology, twentieth-century medicine does not have all the answers, and that there are other, more powerful forces, such as love, that can conquer the unconquerable and defeat the apparently inevitable.

That was, however, an isolated clinical incident – a happy anecdote. Although isolated clinical incidents may impress me, they do not influence truly sceptical scientists, and nor should they. So, for ten or 15 years, the power of love has been ignored by the majority of practising doctors, nurses and other health professionals.

Without proper evidence, no self-respecting clinical teacher would dare suggest that love be considered as powerful a healing tool as penicillin or sulphonamide. However, in the last year or two, evidence has been produced that will in future enable even the most cynical of professional scientists to accept that the power of love does have remarkable healing potential.

Patients with threatening diseases, such as cancer, have a better chance of surviving if they are shown love and affection while they fight their disease.

There is a natural mechanism designed to help ensure that mothers and babies kiss one another frequently. During the last three months of pregnancy, and for 12 months after the birth, a mother's lips produce chemicals designed to make her lips kissable. Sebaceous glands along the borders of the newborn baby's lips produce similar chemicals and help ensure that the baby responds to his/her mother's kisses appropriately.

Unconscious patients in hospital have been brought back to life when played taped messages made by friends and relatives or by people that they respect, admire and love.

Children who are neglected by their parents and deprived of a normal, loving relationship, will suffer in a number of tangible ways.

Babies deprived of a close, loving relationship with their mothers develop more slowly than other babies and stand a greater chance of becoming emotionally unstable.

Insurance companies in the USA have shown that if a wife kisses her husband goodbye when he goes off to work every morning (and murmurs sweet nothings in his ear), he will be less likely to have a car accident on the way to the office or the factory. He will also live about five years longer than his counterpart who does not get a good morning kiss.

At long last the power of love is being officially recognized. Slowly, during the next decade or two, the news will filter through to doctors and hospitals. I have little doubt that in the future doctors will prescribe cuddles three times a day and kisses morning and night.

How to Use the Power of Love in your Life

Do you touch someone you love at least once a day?

NO

You should! Holding hands is good – a cuddle is better. Everyone in your family should start the day with a hug.

YES

Do you tell people you love how you feel about them – regularly?

NO

You should! If you love someone do not be afraid to say it. However secure we are, we all love to be reminded that we are loved.

YES

Do you kiss people you love as often as you can?

NO

You should! A kiss works like a vaccination against unhappiness.

YES

Do you dislike showing signs of affection in public?

YES

NO

Why? There is nothing unnatural about loving someone – or showing it! Our prejudices against showing our love are based on a mixture of unnatural guilt and embarrassment.

Remember, that when you hold his/her hand, stroke his/her hair, clutch him/her to you tightly, whisper in his/her ear and kiss him/her lovingly, you are not just showing that you love him/her – you are also improving his/her life expectation.

When you are away from home or parted from someone you love, do you remind them of your feelings with cards, letters and telephone calls?

NO

You should! However busy you are, you should always find time to keep in touch.

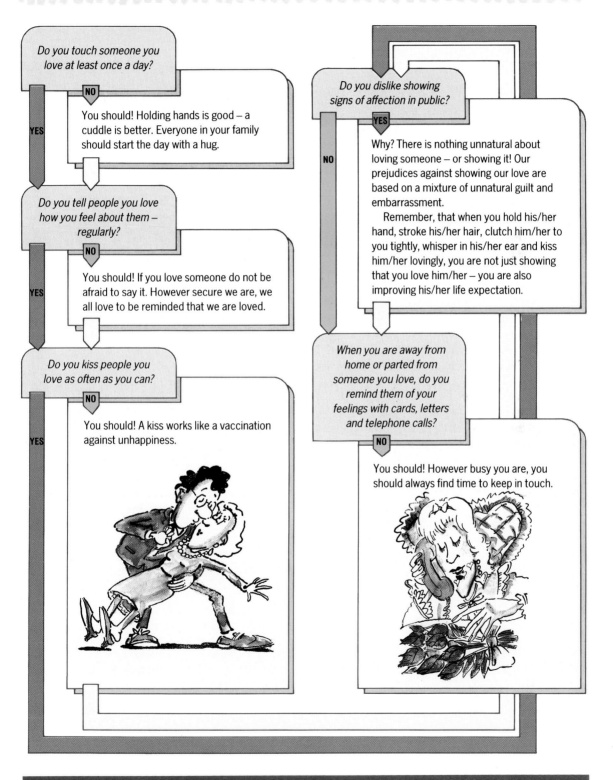

Assertiveness

Thousands of people suffer enormously because they cannot assert themselves. They are pushed around by family, friends, parents, employers, employees, shop assistants, bus drivers, relatives, strangers, doctors – just about everyone they meet. Their lives are run by others.

These unhappy individuals find themselves doing errands for people who could perfectly well run their own errands. They find themselves sitting on committees and doing boring, dull, unrewarding administrative work that no one else wants – invariably for no money. They find themselves burdened with looking after children, while everyone else goes off to have a good time at a nightclub. They find themselves working overtime at weekends and not getting paid for it. They find themselves accepting dinner invitations and other engagements that they would much rather refuse.

In shops, the unassertive will buy things that they do not really need because they have been pressurized by clever salesmen. In cafés, the unassertive will not complain when they have been overcharged. In restaurants, they will not think of returning poorly cooked food. In bus queues, the unassertive will find themselves being pushed out of the way.

In hospital, the unassertive patient will be told to put on his pyjamas and get into bed. He will do as he is told and he will stay in bed, quiet and obedient. The unassertive patient will do what he is told to do, when he is told to do it. He will keep still, will try not to make a nuisance of himself and will not ask too many questions.

Eventually, of course, the unassertive begin to nurse frustrations and hidden anger. They become disenchanted with life and they feel constantly aggrieved. They feel angry with themselves for constantly giving in and they feel angry with those who oppress them. Their anger, inspired by bitterness, eats them up alive. They constantly feel cheated and abused and put upon.

It is hardly surprising that, eventually, the unassertive suffer all sorts of physical and mental ills – inspired by their reluctance to complain or stick up for themselves.

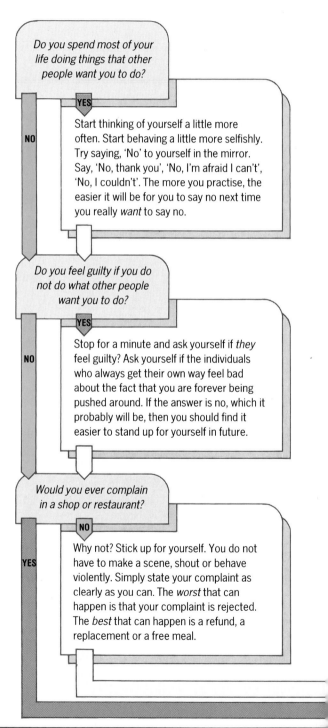

How to Make yourself More Assertive

Do you spend most of your life doing things that other people want you to do?

NO / YES

Start thinking of yourself a little more often. Start behaving a little more selfishly. Try saying, 'No' to yourself in the mirror. Say, 'No, thank you', 'No, I'm afraid I can't', 'No, I couldn't'. The more you practise, the easier it will be for you to say no next time you really *want* to say no.

Do you feel guilty if you do not do what other people want you to do?

NO / YES

Stop for a minute and ask yourself if *they* feel guilty? Ask yourself if the individuals who always get their own way feel bad about the fact that you are forever being pushed around. If the answer is no, which it probably will be, then you should find it easier to stand up for yourself in future.

Would you ever complain in a shop or restaurant?

YES / NO

Why not? Stick up for yourself. You do not have to make a scene, shout or behave violently. Simply state your complaint as clearly as you can. The *worst* that can happen is that your complaint is rejected. The *best* that can happen is a refund, a replacement or a free meal.

If you were forced to go into hospital would you ask questions if you did not understand what was happening to you?

NO

In hospital, the unassertive patient will be put into bed and will stay there: he will do what he is told, when he is told to do it. He will be quiet, keep still and ask no questions. Doctors like their patients to be unassertive because it makes the hospital easier to run. If all the patients keep still and do not ask questions, it makes life easier for the doctors and nurses.

However, the evidence shows that patients who do *not* assert themselves are the first to die. The patients who survive and thrive are the assertive ones who demand information, who refuse to be dominated, who will not accept administrative nonsense (as everyone else does), who want to know the reasons for tests and procedures, who demand to be allowed out of bed as soon as they feel fit.

YES

Do you often get trapped into doing things that you do not want to do?

YES

Be straightforward and honest as often as possible. If you do not want to do something – say so. If you try to offer explanations or excuses, you will probably end up trapping yourself and being manipulated into a corner. For example, if you are invited to a meeting and you try to get out of it by saying that you will be busy that day, you will be trapped if the date of the meeting is changed. You will already have implied that it is only the date that is making it difficult for you to attend.

NO

Do you get flattered into doing things you do not want to do?

YES

People who want you to do something that you do not want to do will often try flattering or praising you – their intention is merely to make you feel bad about saying no. Ignore their false flattery and stand firm.

NO

Do you ever do things you do not want to do because you are frightened of how you will appear to others?

YES

Once you start standing up for yourself, you will find that people treat you with more respect. When you are worried about how others may respond if you stick up for yourself, try to put yourself in their shoes: would you despise someone who told her boss she was not going to work late every night? Would you be appalled if you found that a friend had sent back a meal in a restaurant? Would you think any less of a friend who suddenly decided that she was not going to invite troublesome friends for dinner every fortnight?

NO

Do you ever find yourself trying to solve other people's problems for them – when you do not really want to get involved?

YES

Don't! If someone telephones you and asks you to speak to a group of people that you would rather avoid, you will end up trapping yourself if you start suggesting alternative speakers. The chances are that the people you suggest will either be unavailable or unsuitable. When you can no longer come up with alternatives you will find yourself feeling obliged to accept the invitation! Say 'No, thank you!' clearly, firmly and decisively.

NO

Do you feel that you would have difficulty in sticking up for yourself?

YES

It is not as difficult as you think! You do not have to be aggressive, rude or unpleasant. You simply have to be more aware of your needs and wishes and prepared to stand your ground when you are being put under pressure by others. By learning how to assert yourself, you will gain enormously from the greater self-respect that you will have – and you will have far more time to spend on things you like.

*P*urpose

Without purpose and meaning our lives are hollow and unrewarding. We all need a purpose in our lives – something to hope for, to fight for and to look forward to. With purpose and hope, we can survive almost anything. Purpose, ambition and faith enable us to live through the worst that life can throw at us.

When I was at school, I learnt about the scientist who had dedicated his life to defining the freezing points of gases. After working in his laboratory for many years, he eventually completed his research. He found the freezing point of the last remaining gas. His life's work was complete and he had achieved more than most scientists could ever hope to achieve. But the scientist was not overcome with joy. On the contrary, he became deeply depressed. Within a month or two, he was dead. With his life's work over, there was nothing left for him to live for.

We all need a purpose, a goal, an ambition, an aim or a faith to sustain us on difficult days.

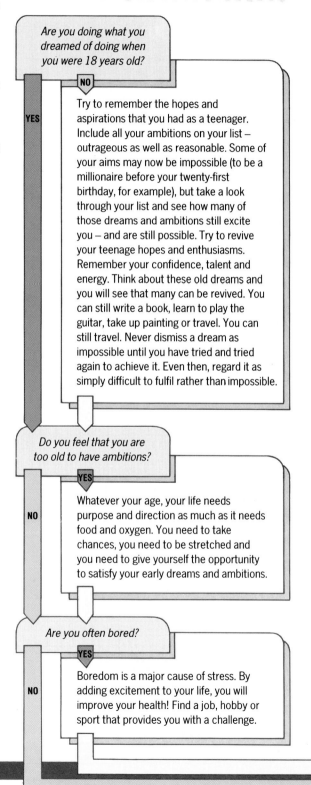

*H*ow to put *P*urpose into your *L*ife

Are you doing what you dreamed of doing when you were 18 years old?

NO → Try to remember the hopes and aspirations that you had as a teenager. Include all your ambitions on your list – outrageous as well as reasonable. Some of your aims may now be impossible (to be a millionaire before your twenty-first birthday, for example), but take a look through your list and see how many of those dreams and ambitions still excite you – and are still possible. Try to revive your teenage hopes and enthusiasms. Remember your confidence, talent and energy. Think about these old dreams and you will see that many can be revived. You can still write a book, learn to play the guitar, take up painting or travel. You can still travel. Never dismiss a dream as impossible until you have tried and tried again to achieve it. Even then, regard it as simply difficult to fulfil rather than impossible.

YES

Do you feel that you are too old to have ambitions?

YES → Whatever your age, your life needs purpose and direction as much as it needs food and oxygen. You need to take chances, you need to be stretched and you need to give yourself the opportunity to satisfy your early dreams and ambitions.

NO

Are you often bored?

YES → Boredom is a major cause of stress. By adding excitement to your life, you will improve your health! Find a job, hobby or sport that provides you with a challenge.

NO

Do you sometimes think that you are wasting your life?

YES

Then make plans now that will make your life more worthwhile. Consider all possibilities – a change of career, emigration, voluntary work or whatever. You must take steps to obtain more responsibility and to give yourself challenges that can be met.

NO

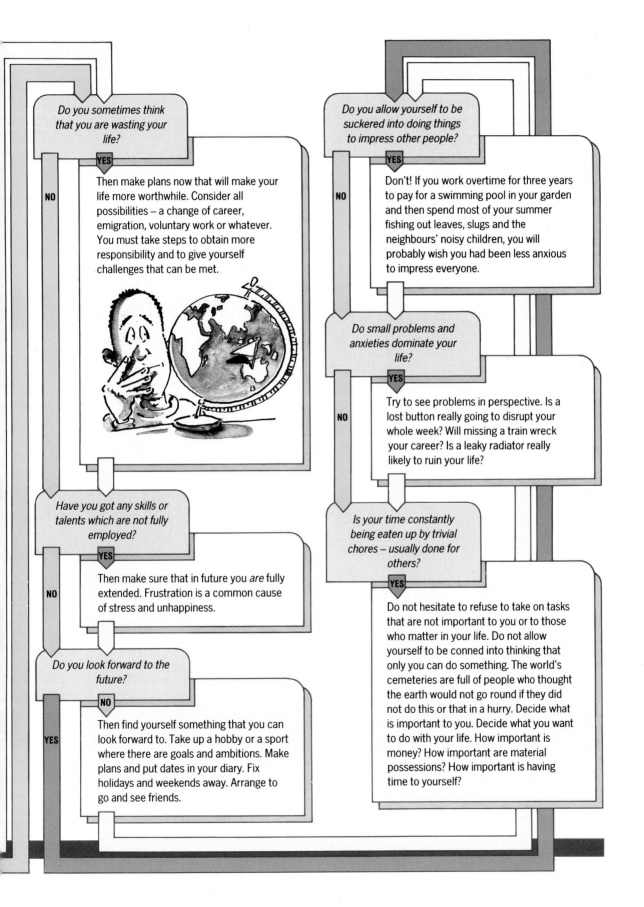

Have you got any skills or talents which are not fully employed?

YES

Then make sure that in future you *are* fully extended. Frustration is a common cause of stress and unhappiness.

NO

Do you look forward to the future?

NO

Then find yourself something that you can look forward to. Take up a hobby or a sport where there are goals and ambitions. Make plans and put dates in your diary. Fix holidays and weekends away. Arrange to go and see friends.

YES

Do you allow yourself to be suckered into doing things to impress other people?

YES

Don't! If you work overtime for three years to pay for a swimming pool in your garden and then spend most of your summer fishing out leaves, slugs and the neighbours' noisy children, you will probably wish you had been less anxious to impress everyone.

NO

Do small problems and anxieties dominate your life?

YES

Try to see problems in perspective. Is a lost button really going to disrupt your whole week? Will missing a train wreck your career? Is a leaky radiator really likely to ruin your life?

NO

Is your time constantly being eaten up by trivial chores – usually done for others?

YES

Do not hesitate to refuse to take on tasks that are not important to you or to those who matter in your life. Do not allow yourself to be conned into thinking that only you can do something. The world's cemeteries are full of people who thought the earth would not go round if they did not do this or that in a hurry. Decide what is important to you. Decide what you want to do with your life. How important is money? How important are material possessions? How important is having time to yourself?

4
How to
Relax Your Mind

ow to

Jardin Publique, by André Lhote, suggests a public garden in its broad use of shape and colour. It is left to the onlooker to reconstruct imaginatively his own idea of the garden's details.

If you have ever watched a film taken by a camera fitted inside a roller coaster car, then you will know how easily your mind can be misled and how your senses can fool your body. As the roller coaster climbs to the top of each rise and then drives rapidly down into the man-made valleys you can feel your stomach churning and your last meal struggling to escape – even though you are sitting very comfortably in a cinema seat. If you are watching the film on television, you may even be sitting in your favourite chair in your own living room. Your body responds not to reality, but to what it thinks is happening.

This phenomenon does not only occur when your mind is being stimulated by a film, of course. Most of us are constantly creating images and scenarios for ourselves simply by thinking and worrying about things. We then invariably respond to our created images and scenarios. If you think that your mild stomach pains might be caused by cancer, they will probably get much worse. If a young girl thinks that her periods are always going to be painful, she will tense her muscles as each period approaches. If you are worried that you are going to lose your job, then your body will respond to your fears – your heart will beat faster, your blood pressure will go up and your muscles will become tense. You will develop a headache not because you have lost your job, but because you are anticipating losing it. Your physical responses are inspired not by reality, but by your imagination.

Under normal circumstances, an almost unceasing flood of impressions pours into your brain. These thoughts, theories and suppositions produce a virtually endless number of assessments, interpretations and anxieties. These are followed, automatically, by physical responses.

Over the last 20 years, many researchers around the world have shown that mental relaxation does work: if you can cut the amount of information that your mind is receiving, you will cut the number of mental responses. By temporarily isolating your brain from stimulating inputs, then you will be temporarily isolated from the need for unnecessary physical responses and your body will relax. You will become rested and and your body will benefit in a number of positive ways. If you suffer from any stress-induced disorder, such as high blood pressure, colitis, asthma, indigestion or eczema, you will benefit enormously. Stress-induced mental problems, such as anxiety or insomnia, will also fade in importance. You will benefit, too, by feeling stronger and healthier and by being more resistant to diseases and disorders of every kind.

Many experts who advocate mental relaxation have favoured meditation, a centuries-old Eastern practice, as a suitable means. For several reasons, meditation techniques discouraged many people from trying to relax their minds. First, those who teach meditation often claim that it is necessary to empty the mind of all thoughts in order to benefit, and that is not easy. Many people find the prospect of emptying their minds completely so daunting that they never even try.

Second, the religious and semi-religious aspects, which seem to be essential to many forms of meditation, frighten many people. Many people would feel terribly self-conscious if they had to sing or chant mystic incantations. The physical aspects of regimes such as yoga frighten many obese or elderly individuals, who would find it difficult or impossible to adopt the positions believed to be essential to this relaxation process.

In fact, you can enjoy all the benefits of mental relaxation without learning how to meditate, joining any religious organization, paying any fees, going into a trance, adopting any strange habits, having your hair shaved off, wearing odd-looking clothes or adopting any uncomfortable postures. All you have to do to stem the flood of potentially harmful sensory information which normally streams into your mind is to learn how to daydream. Or, to be more accurate, to revise your views on daydreaming!

Let a beautiful image like a field of poppies imprint itself on your mind, so that you can retrieve it whenever you need to for peaceful contemplation.

When you were a child, you probably daydreamed regularly, but you may have been taught by your teachers and parents that it is a wasteful, undesirable habit. Children and young people are taught to feel guilty if they slow down. They are told that they are failing themselves and those around them if they sit and watch the world go by for a minute or two. We have been conditioned to think that only by pushing ourselves as hard as possible will we ever achieve anything worthwhile or win the respect of others. Pressured by other people's expectations, we rush through life at top speed, often making ourselves ill by pushing ourselves so hard. We are always in a hurry, hurtling from crisis to crisis and struggling to cram as much as we possibly can into every moment of our lives.

Now, you have to re-learn how to daydream. You must be prepared to allow your imagination to dominate your thinking and to take over your body; you must learn how to structure your imagination so that it allows only peaceful images to fill your mind. If you are going to learn how to daydream effectively, you will have to practise. It is rather like learning how to dance the waltz, drive a car or play golf. If you do not practise, it will never come easily or naturally; the more you practise, the easier it will seem and the better at it you will become.

When you are first re-learning how to daydream, you will need to find somewhere comfortable to lie down. Eventually, you will be able to daydream wherever you are – in a crowded store or on a train, for example – but, to begin with, you need peace and quiet.

If you sit in the garden, you will probably be disturbed by the noises of your neighbour's lawn mower, hedge trimmer or radio. You may spot

weeds that ought to be pulled up, or someone will come round, see you apparently doing nothing in the garden and call in for a drink and a chat. You should choose somewhere quiet and peaceful where you can go easily and regularly, and where you do not expect to be put under any pressure. You need to be alone and away from all distractions. Eventually, you will learn to associate the place you choose with happiness and peacefulness.

If it is daylight, I suggest that you draw the curtains. You need to create a special sort of atmosphere and it is easier to relax in semi-darkness. In addition, the fewer the impulses reaching your senses, the easier you will find relaxation. You may find that lighting a candle helps – both because it will help to create a special atmosphere and because it will give you something to concentrate on. Few things are as soothing as a flickering flame. Similarly, many people find open fires wonderfully hypnotic and relaxing.

The position you choose is up to you. Some people prefer to sit up straight when they are relaxing, in a chair or armchair. Some, of course, favour the lotus position – sitting cross-legged on the ground. For many, stretching out on the sofa or lying down on the bed in the bedroom is probably as good a position or place for relaxing as any. Most important of all is that you feel comfortable.

Daydream 1

You are lying on a warm, sunny beach. It is a day in mid-summer but your beach is absolutely deserted. It is a beautiful place, protected by cliffs from the wind, and you have found a wonderfully secluded sun trap between some rocks. A yacht is

your skin. Your eyes are closed and you can feel the sun on your eyelids. It is not at all stifling or unbearable, rather you find it exquisitely restful to be bathed so totally in warmth. You have oiled yourself carefully with sun lotion to protect yourself from the burning effect of the sun's rays and you can smell the lotion.

If you opened your eyes, you would be able to see your skin glistening in the sunshine. However, the sun is quite bright on your eyelids and you do not want

Wherever you choose, try to make sure that you will not be disturbed. Take the telephone off the hook or switch on your answering machine if you have one. Put a 'Do not disturb' notice on the outside of the door and close and lock the door to the room you have chosen.

Once you feel comfortable, your first task is to regulate your breathing. Start by breathing in deeply, mentally counting up to four while you do it. Then hold your breath for a count of two. Breathe out, again counting up to four. When you have emptied your lungs, hold that position for another count of two and then start the whole process again by taking another deep breath in. You will find that breathing deeply helps you to get your body and your mind into a gentle state of relaxation. If unwanted and distracting thoughts and worries pop into your mind, write them down on a piece of paper. The problems and difficulties of the everyday world can wait for a few minutes.

As you relax, try to conjure up a restful scene that will help you relax completely – a daydream to wander in where you can find peace and tranquillity. I have prepared a series of daydreams for you to follow to start with but, as the weeks go by (and when you are learning how to relax you need to practise regularly, preferably daily), you can build up a library of your own favourite, private daydreams.

anchored out at sea and you can hear faint laughter and the tinkling of glasses. Occasionally, there is a splash as someone dives off the boat into the water. The noises are very distant. High, high overhead you can hear seagulls calling. Just a few yards away, the sea is breaking on the sandy shore. The rhythmic sound of the breaking waves is remarkably soothing.

The most insistent sensation is that of warmth. The sand underneath you is warm; the sun is warm on

to open your eyes just yet. You lie there, quite still and peaceful, soaking up the sun and enjoying the afternoon warmth.

*D*aydream 2

Imagine that you are walking along a pleasant country lane in early summer. The narrow lane is quite deserted and you are completely alone. On either side of you, the hedgerows are overgrown and full of colourful wild flowers. Beyond the hedges stretch meadows of green grass, decorated only with dazzling,

blue tits and yellow-hammers. Every so often, there is an oak tree standing in the hedgerow. Each time you come to a tree you stand for a few moments and relax in its shade. On one occasion, you glance casually through a gap in the hedge and your eyes fall on a hare playing just a few feet inside the meadow. It seems

particularly soft and especially green; it is mixed with moss and clover and has a delightfully springy texture. You look around, find a place where you can sit with your back leaning against a tree and settle down with the stream chattering busily to itself no more than a foot from your feet. In the water, you can

yellow buttercups and red poppies dancing lightly in the gentlest of summer breezes. The sky is blue, dotted only with a few small, fluffy white clouds. The sunshine is wonderfully warm.

As you walk along the lane, you can hear dozens of different birds singing and you can see sparrows, blackbirds, thrushes, wrens,

oblivious to your presence and you watch it, noiselessly, for several minutes.

When you started your walk, the lane seemed to stretch far, far into the distance. You could see no sign of its ending. Now you notice that it is about to descend into a pleasant, lightly wooded valley. Just before the lane starts to

slope downwards, you come to a narrow stone bridge. It crosses a clear stream that splashes its way across a mass of round, water-smoothed pebbles.

You stop for a moment, see that there is a narrow path leading down to the stream, and clamber down it until you are standing on the bank. The grass here is

see a small river trout looking for food. On the opposite bank, where the stream widens, a kingfisher sits, waiting to dart. From a little further upstream, you hear a light splash and catch a glimpse of an otter diving into deeper water.

You sit, comfortable, relaxed and calm. The world seems a million, million miles

away. Your worries and anxieties are forgotten; compared with what is around you, nothing seems important. This is real, and the rest of the world is only a half-forgotten memory. You close your eyes. Now you can only just hear the stream. You relax even further and feel your cares falling from your shoulders.

Daydream 3

You are sitting in a bedroom in a large, comfortable and rather expensive country hotel. The cost of the room does not concern you in the slightest. You have no worries about money, you have as much as you need. You are wearing nothing but a dressing gown tied loosely around your waist as you sit in a comfortable, leather armchair watching a crackling log fire. Occasionally, you move forward just far enough to throw on another log.

The weather is freezing cold, but the temperature in your bedroom is comfortably warm. You spent the morning walking across the hills and you can still remember the bite of the

the only other customers were a few colourful regulars who greeted you distantly but politely. The food there was excellent – all the better for your being hungry after your long walk in cold air. After lunch, you walked back to your hotel along a different path. You arrived back an hour or so ago.

You had a piping hot bath in an old-fashioned bathroom. The bath was so large that you could float. After drying yourself on a massive, soft, fluffy white towel, you put on your dressing gown, rang the hotel reception and asked for a tray of tea and some muffins to be sent up. Now you sit by the fire and you smile contentedly, for life seems very good.

leaded window with thick, red velvet curtains hanging on each side of it. If you turned your head to the right, you would be able to look through the window at the corner of a beautiful and peaceful garden. In the distance, you would be able to see countless acres of rolling countryside. There is a lake, a stone folly and a small wood. In front of the window, there is a long seat covered in fabric that matches the red velvet curtains.

The door to your room is on your left and almost impossible to distinguish from the walls. It is made of exactly the same sort of rich oak as the panelling. A large, old-fashioned iron key protrudes from the lock and

cool, winter air. The mud tracks in the rough lane leading to the path across the hills were frozen solid, and you had the satisfaction of crunching your way through countless frozen puddles on the track. While you were out, you had lunch in a traditional, old-fashioned inn a few miles from the hotel. The inn was quiet and

Behind you there is a four-poster, hung with a brocade canopy made of a rich red and gold material. Matching curtains hang at all four corners of the bed and are tied back with red ropes, fastened in neat bows.

The room is panelled in oak and there is one window on your right. It is an old-fashioned, diamond-paned,

the bolt has been drawn as an added, though unnecessary, precaution.

By your side, on the arm of your chair, you have a book that you are enjoying and a copy of a favourite magazine. You know that the chef downstairs will be preparing your dinner. You are in no hurry; there is plenty of time for you to

enjoy the moment, to savour the peace and to relax thoroughly and completely.

You lean back in your chair and close your eyes. You can still see the dancing flames of the log fire. What more can you ask?

*D*aydream 4

You are on the Venice Simplon-Orient-Express heading for Venice. You have a compartment of your own and for the next 24 hours, you have nothing to worry about, nowhere else to go, no work, no telephone calls,

player and you suspect that it will be a challenging and exciting game. At the moment you are resting in your compartment, enjoying the unashamed luxury of the expensive fittings.

Dinner really was quite spectacular. You have enjoyed many fine meals, but you have never eaten or drunk so well in your life. The service was excellent – polite but never intrusive, efficient but never cold. And there was something undeniably exciting about

enjoying a meal on the train that has starred in so many books and films.

Suddenly, your mind flashes back to Paris. You have just spent three weeks there at a splendid hotel right in the heart of the city. You passed your final evening having dinner at a magnificent restaurant and wandering up and down the Champs-Élysées with a friend you met at the hotel. You are on your way to spend ten days in Venice and then you will be returning to Paris. You

motion of the train is threatening to send you to sleep. It is just beginning to snow again and you suspect that, within an hour or two, the fields through which your train is passing will be carpeted in white. You are glad you brought a warm coat with you, even though it

is gloriously cosy in your compartment. You know that, at this time of the year, Venice can sometimes be rather chilly.

You look at your watch. You have 20 minutes before you are due to meet your

no pressures, no anxieties – nothing. You are free to relax and enjoy yourself.

About an hour ago you finished dinner – a splendid meal – and three other passengers, with whom you had exchanged pleasantries, invited you to join them for liqueurs and a game of cards. They seemed an interesting trio and you said that you would be delighted. You agreed to meet in the Bar Car in half an hour or so. You are an excellent card

have promised to meet your friend again on your first evening back in the French capital and have booked a table at Maxim's.

Meanwhile, you are looking forward to Venice. It is a city you know well. The hotel where you always stay has your usual suite reserved for you. The manager and most of the staff know you by name and are familiar with your preferences. You will have dinner with many old friends. You will walk through the city, relax in a gondola and enjoy the spirit of the centuries. You may take a river taxi across to the Lido and wander along the shore there. You will see friends in Harry's Bar. You will lie in and have long, leisurely breakfasts at your hotel. Your suite overlooks the lagoon and you can watch the boats scurrying about while you enjoy your croissants and coffee.

But that is tomorrow. Today, the combination of the excellent claret you had at dinner and the gentle

travelling companions. You decide that you will just lie down for a while and have a snooze. You settle back in your compartment and close your eyes.

Daydream 5

It is winter in St Moritz. You are staying in your favourite hotel. You always spend three weeks there in mid-winter. It is lunchtime and you are sitting in a mountain-top café having lunch. You feel good.

After a splendid breakfast in the hotel dining room, you collected your skis and boots from the basement and took the lift up to the top of a mountain. From there you took a run that you always enjoy. It is never dangerous but always invigorating. The track leads down the mountain between the trees, giving you wonderful views of the valley below. Sometimes the mountain is crowded, but today it is quiet. You see a few familiar faces but there

are no crowds and no queues at all in the cafés or at the ski lift.

You have chosen something light for lunch. You are planning another long run this afternoon. You will ski down the other side of the mountain before taking the lift back to the top and then returning to your

hotel. You know that dinner this evening will, as usual, be magnificent. When you get back to the hotel, you will have a warm, deep bath at leisure. There are few joys more complete than a relaxing bath after a good day's skiing.

Sitting in the café, you feel warm and comfortable. The sun coming through the windows is warm and soothing. You close your eyes for a moment and feel refreshed and relaxed. You have nothing but pleasure on your mind.

Daydreams can be based on reality, taken from films, television programmes or books, or purely imaginary. It does not matter where you get your daydreams from as long as you find them credible. If you think that you will have difficulty in creating daydreams for yourself, collect postcards, holiday snaps, calendar pictures or holiday brochures. Look at your photograph or postcard through half-closed eyes; try to remember all the relevant sensations, the sounds, the smells, the temperature and so on. Try to envisage yourself there. In future, when you go on holiday, collect postcards or take photographs of all the places that you find comfortable and calming. Find special, secret, personal places which you can associate with relaxation.

As a form of relaxation daydreaming is just as good as meditation and has one great advantage over it. With meditation, you have to empty your mind completely and replace very real anxieties with a perfectly empty space. That is not easy to do. With daydreaming, however, you replace your natural fears with calming, comfortable, tranquil memories which themselves have a positive, calming effect. When you fill the void in your mind with thoughts, you do not simply arrest the damage, you build up your strength with positive, health-giving feelings.

If you want proof of just how relaxing daydreaming can be, I suggest that you take your pulse at the start of a session and again at the end. (You will find your pulse in your wrist, just below the base of your thumb. Use the fingers of the opposite hand to feel for it.) You will almost certainly notice a fall in your pulse rate after a ten or 15 minute daydreaming session – ample proof that this type of relaxation technique does work and really can help protect your body from stress.

Try not to get into the habit of checking your pulse, however. Daydreaming is not a competitive exercise and you will not benefit properly if you are forever worrying about whether you have managed to bring your pulse rate down.

Two words of warning: first, you should never, of course, try daydreaming while you are driving a car or operating any machinery and, second, do not get up suddenly after a daydreaming session. If you have relaxed well, your blood pressure will probably have fallen considerably and if you do get up too quickly, you may feel dizzy. Stretch your legs and arms carefully and gently for a minute or two and then move slowly into an upright position. It may even be a good idea to hold on to something while you stand up.

Once you have learned how to daydream properly, you will be able to use the technique wherever you are and whatever you are doing (bearing the above restrictions in mind). If you are sitting or standing on a crowded train, you will be able to disappear to one of your favourite daydream haunts and escape from the noise and the bustle. If you are in the dentist's chair, you will be able to take yourself away from the pain and discomfort to a soothing place where you can lie in the sun. If you are queuing in a busy shop waiting for attention, you will be able to relax your mind and your body by disappearing for a few seconds to a country hideout. You will be able to replace the very real, damaging frustrations of the world with the feelings you derive from a scene that you find soothing, calming and relaxing.

5
Use Your Intuition

There are no prizes for guessing where the fortunes of these three clowns ended up. Nevertheless there are numerous off-screen stories of people who have dreamed the name of the Derby winner or foreseen extraordinary events.

One of the few things we know for certain about the human mind is that we cannot define its limits. Just half a generation or so ago, most reputable scientists dismissed extra-sensory perception and telepathy as pseudo-scientific mumbo jumbo. You would have had difficulty finding any Nobel Prize-winner or professor of science prepared to admit publicly that there may be a sixth sense.

I suspect that, today, you would have just as much difficulty finding any Nobel Prize-winning scientist or professor of science prepared to state categorically that neither telepathy nor extra-sensory perception can possibly exist. In the USA, the Pentagon has invested millions of dollars in investigating parapsychology and the Federal Bureau of Investigation has been known to hire psychics to help solve crimes. In addition, hundreds of leading industrialists and politicians have sought professional and personal advice from those who have awe-inspiring mental powers.

As it becomes more acceptable for ordinary people to admit to having had what can only be described as 'unreal' experiences, so it becomes clear that the mind can operate in very mysterious ways. Too many individuals have had dreams – and then discovered that their dreams meant something – for these powers to be dismissed. The mind, it now seems clear, can work in remarkable ways.

I had an experience which can only be described as exceptional about 18 months ago. At the time, I lived in a cottage on the cliffs between the twin North Devon villages of Lynton and Lynmouth. The villages are probably about as isolated as any in England – the nearest traffic lights are over 20 miles away and the nearest mainline railway station is just over 40 miles away, in Taunton.

I used the railway station at Taunton quite regularly to go to London, and I always enjoyed the drive back across Exmoor and along the coast to Lynton. At night, apart from during the short holiday season, there was very little traffic on the coast road and the views across the moors and the Bristol Channel were breathtaking.

At about nine o'clock one winter evening, I was about five or six miles away from Lynton when I drove around a bend and saw that the whole of the sky above where I knew the village to be situated was bright

How well Developed are your Powers of Intuition?

Most of us have intuitive skills that we use too infrequently. By taking greater advantage of these skills we could often deal with daily problems with far less stress than normal.

Before you can use your powers of intuition, you must be aware that you have them! Answer the questions which follow and find out just how strong your sense of intuition really is.

1 How many times have you 'known' who was on the other end of a telephone before picking up the receiver?

(a) never
(b) once
(c) twice or more
      (Exclude those times when you could reasonably have expected to guess who was calling.)

2 How many times have you thought about someone you had not heard from for ages and then, quite unexpectedly, received a telephone call, letter or postcard from him/her?

(a) never
(b) once
(c) twice or more

3 How many times have you known what was in a letter before opening it — and been right?

(a) never
(b) once
(c) twice or more

4 How well do you do in guessing games?

(a) very well
(b) average
(c) not very well

5 Have you ever heard voices telling you what to do?

(a) yes
(b) no

6 How often do you act on a hunch?

(a) never
(b) occasionally
(c) often

7 How many times have you had bad dreams which turned out to be true?

(a) often
(b) never
(c) occasionally

8 How many times have you won a bet on a hunch?

(a) never
(b) occasionally
(c) often

9 How often do you make good, snap decisions about people you meet?

(a) never
(b) occasionally
(c) often

10 Do you think you instinctively know when things are going to work well or fail?

(a) yes
(b) no

Check your Score!

1	(a) 1	(b) 2	(c) 3
2	(a) 1	(b) 2	(c) 3
3	(a) 3	(b) 2	(c) 1
4	(a) 1	(b) 2	(c) 3
5	(a) 3	(b) 1	
6	(a) 1	(b) 2	(c) 3
7	(a) 3	(b) 1	(c) 2
8	(a) 1	(b) 2	(c) 3
9	(a) 1	(b) 2	(c) 3
10	(a) 3	(b) 1	

If you scored 11 or more, you have intuitive powers that you could use to your advantage. The greater your score, the greater your powers. If you scored between 25 and 30, your intuitive powers are extremely impressive.

orange and red with flames. There was no doubt in my mind that there was a major fire in the village. It was a terrifying sight and I increased my speed in order to get home as soon as possible. As I drove, I tried to keep my eye on the flames as much as I could. Occasionally, as the road twisted and turned, I lost sight of the fire and the lighted-up sky, but, whenever I was in a position to see the hill above the village, the flames were clear and bright.

Even though I was driving quickly, it took me seven or eight minutes to cross the moors from the place where I had first seen the flames to the top of Countisbury Hill, where I could see the villages of Lynton and Lynmouth. I slowed down as I reached the top of the hill, hoping that I could see where the fire was situated. I knew that, since the village was 20 miles away from the nearest town, Barnstaple, it would take at least half an hour for full fire-fighting crews to reach the scene. There is a part-time crew in Lynton, but the size of the blaze seemed to suggest that it would be beyond their capabilities. Neither is there a proper hospital in Lynton – just a cottage hospital and one ambulance – and I was concerned for the welfare of the villagers.

When I reached the top of Countisbury Hill, I expected to see at least 10 or 20 houses ablaze. I expected to see that the trees on the hill separating Lynton from Lynmouth had caught fire and that the large, old-fashioned hotels that make up most of the trade in the villages were on fire too. The flames that I had seen had been terrifying. Even from several miles away they had suggested that a major fire was spreading rapidly through the village.

Strangely, from the top of Countisbury Hill, I could see nothing. No flames, no fire, no devastation – nothing. The villages looked just as sleepy and peaceful as ever. The flames had gone and the fire had disappeared. I was astonished, relieved and happy and, selfishly, I was particularly pleased that my own home and those in it were not touched by the flames I thought I had seen.

I was puzzled, too, and the next morning, when I went to collect my newspaper, I asked whether there had been any fires in the village the previous night. The newsagent shook his head. There had been nothing that he knew of, and he knew most things that happened in the village. I told him that I thought I had seen flames coming from the village. The source of the fire, I explained, seemed to me to have been some houses on the hill behind the village.

The local man nodded wisely. 'Hollerday Hill,' he said. I looked at him, slightly confused.

'The big house on Hollerday Hill,' he went on. I waited. 'It burned down,' he finished.

'Is that the hill right behind the town?' I asked him.

A nod.

'It looked like a big blaze,' I said.

'It was a massive house,' agreed the newsagent. 'It was owned by Sir George Newnes, the publisher. Massive country house. But it burned down to the ground.'

'Was anyone hurt?' I asked, anxiously.

The newsagent screwed up his eyes and thought for a few moments.

'Do you know I can't remember,' he said. He suggested that if I really wanted to know about the fire in any detail I should ask one of the village's older residents.

'But you must know!' I insisted. 'And what happened to the ambulances and the fire engines? Everyone in the village must have been there.'

The newsagent looked at me as if I had lost my senses. 'I don't know whether they had any ambulances there,' he said. He seemed puzzled by my suggestions.

But still I did not understand. 'It must have been the biggest fire Lynton has ever had,' I said.

How to Use your Intuition

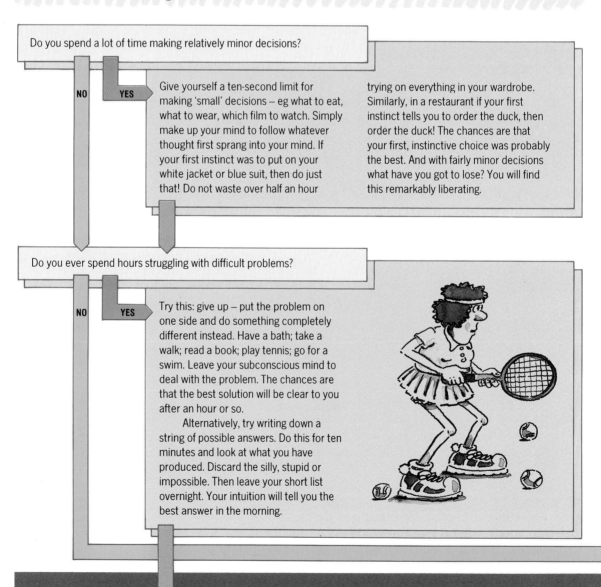

Do you spend a lot of time making relatively minor decisions?

NO   YES

Give yourself a ten-second limit for making 'small' decisions – eg what to eat, what to wear, which film to watch. Simply make up your mind to follow whatever thought first sprang into your mind. If your first instinct was to put on your white jacket or blue suit, then do just that! Do not waste over half an hour trying on everything in your wardrobe. Similarly, in a restaurant if your first instinct tells you to order the duck, then order the duck! The chances are that your first, instinctive choice was probably the best. And with fairly minor decisions what have you got to lose? You will find this remarkably liberating.

Do you ever spend hours struggling with difficult problems?

NO   YES

Try this: give up – put the problem on one side and do something completely different instead. Have a bath; take a walk; read a book; play tennis; go for a swim. Leave your subconscious mind to deal with the problem. The chances are that the best solution will be clear to you after an hour or so.

Alternatively, try writing down a string of possible answers. Do this for ten minutes and look at what you have produced. Discard the silly, stupid or impossible. Then leave your short list overnight. Your intuition will tell you the best answer in the morning.

The newsagent nodded with more certainty but said nothing.

'But you're acting as though it doesn't concern you,' I said. 'There must have been people there that you know!' I was quite mystified by how little he seemed to know about the incident – and slightly perturbed that he appeared to care very little for his friends and fellow villagers.

By this time the newsagent looked really puzzled by what I was saying. 'I didn't know anyone who was there,' he insisted. 'My grandfather might have done I suppose.'

'Your grandfather!' I exclaimed. 'Why?'

'Well, it did burn down well over 50 years ago,' said the newsagent. 'Hollerday House has been a burnt-out wreck for over half a century.'

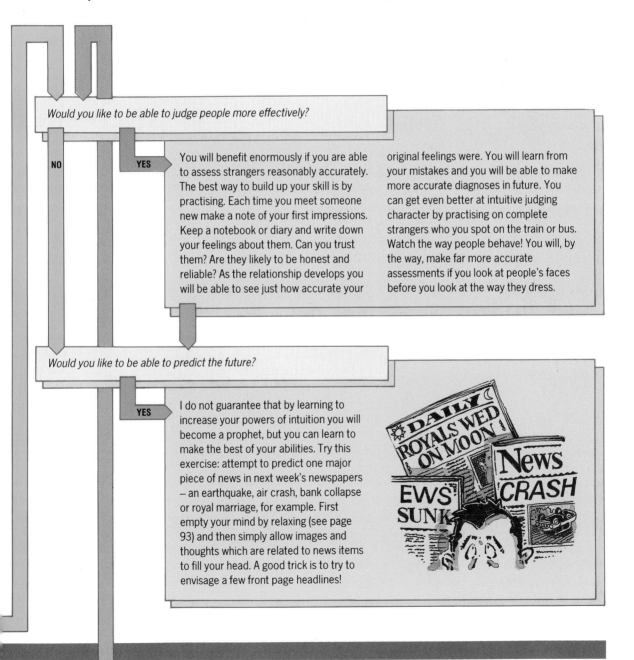

Would you like to be able to judge people more effectively?

NO   **YES**

You will benefit enormously if you are able to assess strangers reasonably accurately. The best way to build up your skill is by practising. Each time you meet someone new make a note of your first impressions. Keep a notebook or diary and write down your feelings about them. Can you trust them? Are they likely to be honest and reliable? As the relationship develops you will be able to see just how accurate your original feelings were. You will learn from your mistakes and you will be able to make more accurate diagnoses in future. You can get even better at intuitive judging character by practising on complete strangers who you spot on the train or bus. Watch the way people behave! You will, by the way, make far more accurate assessments if you look at people's faces before you look at the way they dress.

Would you like to be able to predict the future?

YES

I do not guarantee that by learning to increase your powers of intuition you will become a prophet, but you can learn to make the best of your abilities. Try this exercise: attempt to predict one major piece of news in next week's newspapers – an earthquake, air crash, bank collapse or royal marriage, for example. First empty your mind by relaxing (see page 93) and then simply allow images and thoughts which are related to news items to fill your head. A good trick is to try to envisage a few front page headlines!

6

Use Your Mind
to Control Stress

Travelling in the rush-hour with the noise and pollution of a crowded city, modern man lives in a stressful environment. You need to use your imagination to teach your body to relax.

Stress is the greatest environmental hazard of our time. I doubt if there is a doctor anywhere who does not accept that stress (by which I mean anything that causes fear, anxiety, worry, apprehension, anger or even excitement) can cause quite genuine physical responses and very real diseases. The figures vary from report to report, but at a conservative estimate, at least three-quarters of the illnesses treated by doctors are completely or largely psychosomatic in origin. As I said earlier in this book, I estimate that between 90 and 95 per cent of all illnesses can be blamed wholly or mainly on stress.

Consider the common headache. It is true that some headaches are caused by injuries and brain tumours, but experts agree that at least 98 per cent of all headaches are stress- and pressure-related. When under stress, we screw up our eyes and tense the muscles around our heads – and we get headaches.

Or take indigestion – one of the most usual disorders known to twentieth-century man. It is so common that, if five people sit down to dinner, the chances are that at least one of them will have stomach pains afterwards. Occasionally, indigestion may be caused by poor eating habits or by eating the wrong sort of food, but, in the vast majority of cases, it is caused by anxiety.

Even when indigestion seems to be caused by bad eating habits, it is often easy to show the root cause to be stress. When a salesman hurries his lunch, he is probably hurrying because he is under stress. When a woman grabs a sandwich while she works at her desk, it is more than possible that she is feeling anxious about her work. When an office manager swallows food without chewing, it is probably because he is desperate to get back to work and sort out an accumulation of problems.

Although there seems to be absolutely no doubt that stress is killing many people, there is one important question that has to be asked: *why* are we so susceptible to stress these days? If you think about it carefully, you might imagine that we should have good, stress-free lives. Most of us have somewhere warm and dry to sleep at night, we get enough to eat, we do not have to worry too much about being eaten by wild animals, we can obtain light and heat at the flick of a switch, we can obtain water simply by turning on a tap, we have central heating, cars, bank accounts and so many material goods that we buy one another all sorts of unnecessary rubbish at Christmas time.

It is not difficult to understand why our ancestors suffered from stress. They had to worry about staying alive, finding somewhere dry and warm to sleep at night and getting enough to eat. Compared to them, we have an easy life. Stress *ought* to be the last thing troubling us and yet stress is the twentieth-century equivalent of the plague.

The answer to this paradox is quite simple. Our bodies were designed a long time ago. We were not designed for the sort of world in which we live today, but for one in which running and fighting were essential, practical solutions to real, everyday problems. We were designed to cope with a predominantly physical world, and we are, I fear, sadly out of date. The trouble is that we have changed our world far more rapidly than our bodies have been able to adapt. Revolutionary changes in navigation,

How we Should have Changed for Life in the

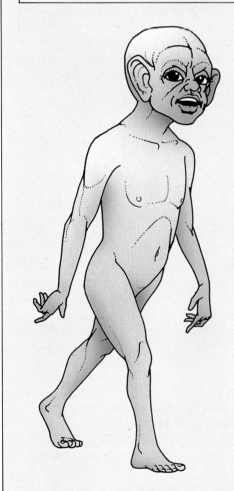

- We do not need to be as tall or as broad as we are. Nor do we need to be designed for hard physical work. Humans could comfortably be about 4 feet tall and about 6 stones in weight.

- Our legs have a rudimentary role – we use wheeled transport for most of our moving about. Our legs could be much shorter in comparison to our overall size.

- There is no need for differences of musculature between the sexes – men and women do similar work these days.

- We do not need hair to keep us warm – body hair, head hair, facial hair and pubic hair could all disappear. We could all be completely bald.

- Mass movement of populations means that variations in skin colour are irrelevant. We should all be dark brown in colour to protect us from the harmful rays of the sun. Since most of us wear clothes most of the time, it would probably be appropriate for us to have brown hands and faces, while our bodies and limbs should be white.

- There is no need for there to be any obvious physical differences between the sexes. The industry, medicine, communications, transport and military techniques mean that our world has been transformed, but our bodies have changed very little in the last 10,000 years. It takes millions of years for the human body to adapt to its changing environment. In short, we have moved far too quickly for our own good.

Imagine that you are a caveman or -woman. You and your mate live in a cave which you share with another primitive couple and a cluster of assorted children of questionable parentage. Each day you face the same routine problems. You have to get hold of enough wood to keep your fire burning, you have to avoid being eaten, you have to find enough food to stay alive, and you have to make the odd piece of clothing to keep out the worst of the winter chill. The daily problems are fundamental, simple and very straightforward. Your expectations, needs, ambitions and pressures are easily defined.

Every problem that you face will either be solved quickly by a

21st Century

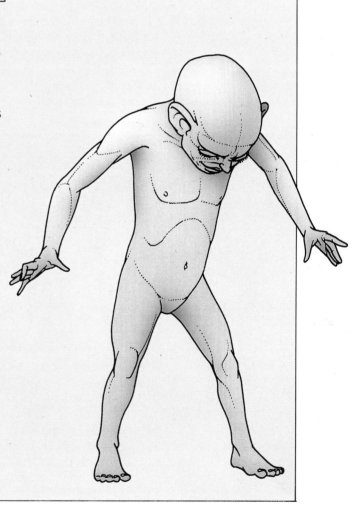

human population is in no danger of dying out and we have killed off or controlled our predators so successfully that our main danger to ourselves is over-reproducing. Most of the obvious differences between the sexes could disappear – leaving us with small sexual organs as the only difference. Women could have breasts which developed only towards the end of pregnancy.

● Our hands and feet should be smaller – so that we can more easily operate machines and computers.

● We do not need to respond quickly to crises. We would be much healthier if we produced less adrenalin when under stress.

● Our ears and eyes need to be slightly more powerful to begin with to allow for the effects of ageing. Our ear lobes and ears should, therefore, perhaps be larger. (More and more people live to be old and to have trouble with their hearing and vision.)

● Most of the food we eat is mushy and does not need biting. Our teeth are, therefore, unnecessary. Hard gums would be just as efficient and would cause far less trouble.

physical response or it will not be solved at all. When you find yourself face to face with a pack of hungry wolves, your heart will beat faster, your blood pressure will go up, your muscles will tense and acid will pour into your stomach. All these sound physiological responses will help you to stay alive by increasing your chances of fighting or escaping. When your muscles tense, you will be better equipped for fighting or running away. When extra blood is pumped around your body, you will be better able to move quickly and efficiently. When the acid pours into your stomach, any food lying there will quickly be turned into valuable energy.

Compare this existence to life today. Think yourself through a fairly ordinary, routine sort of day. You wake up in your well-decorated bedroom and your first problem is deciding what to wear. You have a wardrobe that contains enough clothes for a family! You wash in hot water that comes straight out of the tap. You cook yourself breakfast by turning on the electric kettle, putting bread in the electric toaster and boiling an egg on the stove. As you eat, you read your daily newspaper.

It sounds an easy, well-regulated sort of life-style. But there are problems. You see from your newspaper that interest rates are rising. That means that your repayments to the bank will have to go up. In your morning mail you get a number of bills that you cannot pay and an invitation to dinner with people you cannot stand. As you struggle through your breakfast, worrying about these problems, you feel a headache developing and the beginnings of the day's first bout of indigestion.

When you get into the car to go to work, you suddenly remember that you have not filled it up with petrol – and you have to be at a meeting

Stress may impinge on family life through practical worries about bills and rising interest rates, social obligations or worries about the day ahead.

60 miles away within an hour and a half. You switch on the ignition but the car will not start – the battery is flat. When, eventually, you get it started, you discover that the main route to your office is jammed solid with cars and lorries. The local council is doing roadworks and the hold-ups seem to be going on for ever. You are overtaken by a cyclist who breaks off your radio aerial as he rides past. His handlebars make a long scratch down the side of your car, damaging the paintwork. You are, however, prevented by the neighbouring cars in the traffic jam from getting out and chasing after him.

Finally arriving at the office, you discover a thousand separate problems. A colleague is away sick, a memo from a boss doubles your workload, there are rumours of new appointments and talk of the Chairman coming to look around the offices next week.

And so it goes on – every minute of every day is filled with problems, anxieties, worries and crises. The problems do not threaten your life, but they do threaten your *way* of life; they threaten you. As a result, your body responds to each new threat in the same, old-fashioned, physical way. When you open a telephone bill, your blood pressure will go up, your heart will beat faster, your muscles will tense, and acid will pour into your stomach. You respond to every new problem, threat and imagined threat in exactly the same way that your ancestor would have responded to the appearance of a pack of wolves.

Stress surrounds us every day. We have created a world in which pressure is inescapable. Our bodies' constant attempts to deal with the threat of daily pressures result in the development of a wide range of genuine physical and mental disorders.

Late for work on an already crises-filled day, a traffic jam can be a threat to your sense of order and stability.

Is Stress Affecting your Health?

The biggest myth about stress is that it is, by itself, a killer. The truth is that stress itself never killed anyone. It is the way we respond to stress that does the damage. Some people respond well and can cope with enormous amounts of stress. Others respond badly – and fall ill when they have to endure quite small amounts of stress.

This specially prepared flow chart will help you check your *personal* exposure to stress and your *personal* susceptibility to stress. First, find out how much stress there is in your life. Next, work out how vulnerable you are to stress. Then, discover whether you are a potential stress victim.

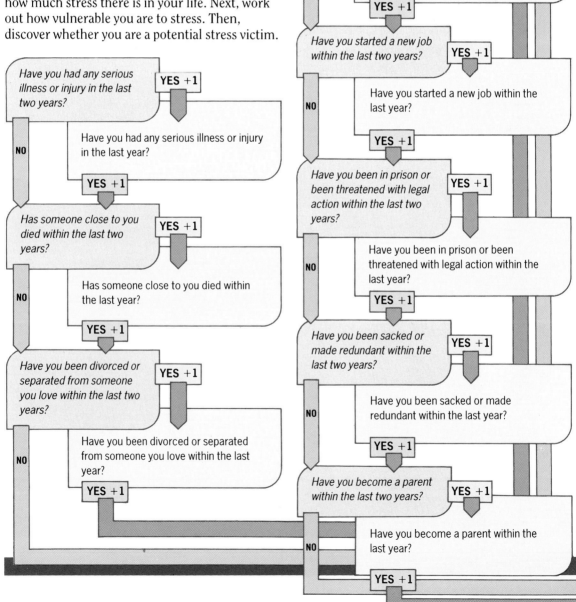

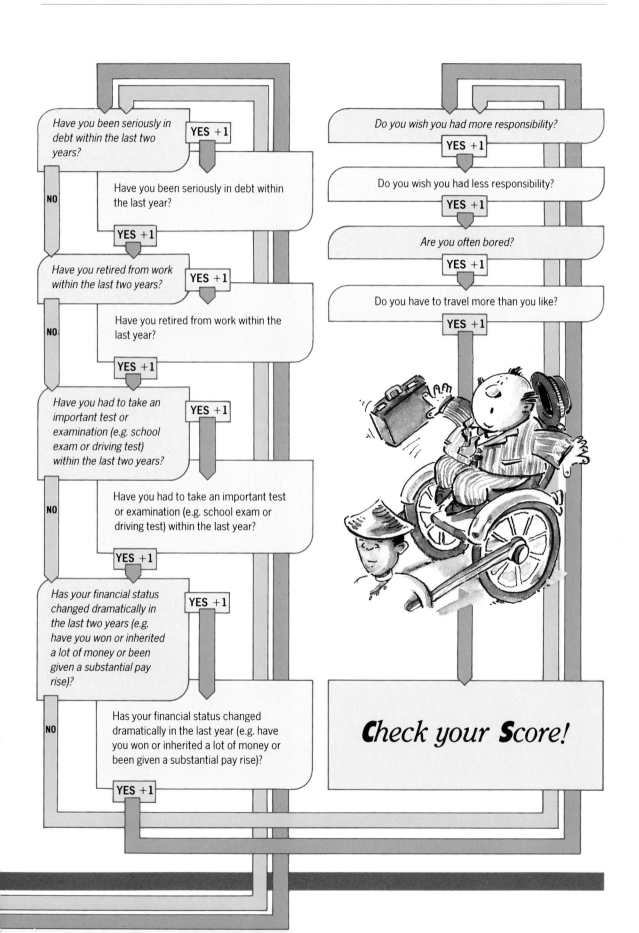

Have you been seriously in debt within the last two years?

YES +1

NO

Have you been seriously in debt within the last year?

YES +1

Have you retired from work within the last two years?

YES +1

NO

Have you retired from work within the last year?

YES +1

Have you had to take an important test or examination (e.g. school exam or driving test) within the last two years?

YES +1

NO

Have you had to take an important test or examination (e.g. school exam or driving test) within the last year?

YES +1

Has your financial status changed dramatically in the last two years (e.g. have you won or inherited a lot of money or been given a substantial pay rise)?

YES +1

NO

Has your financial status changed dramatically in the last year (e.g. have you won or inherited a lot of money or been given a substantial pay rise)?

YES +1

Do you wish you had more responsibility?

YES +1

Do you wish you had less responsibility?

YES +1

Are you often bored?

YES +1

Do you have to travel more than you like?

YES +1

Check your Score!

How Susceptible are you to Stress?

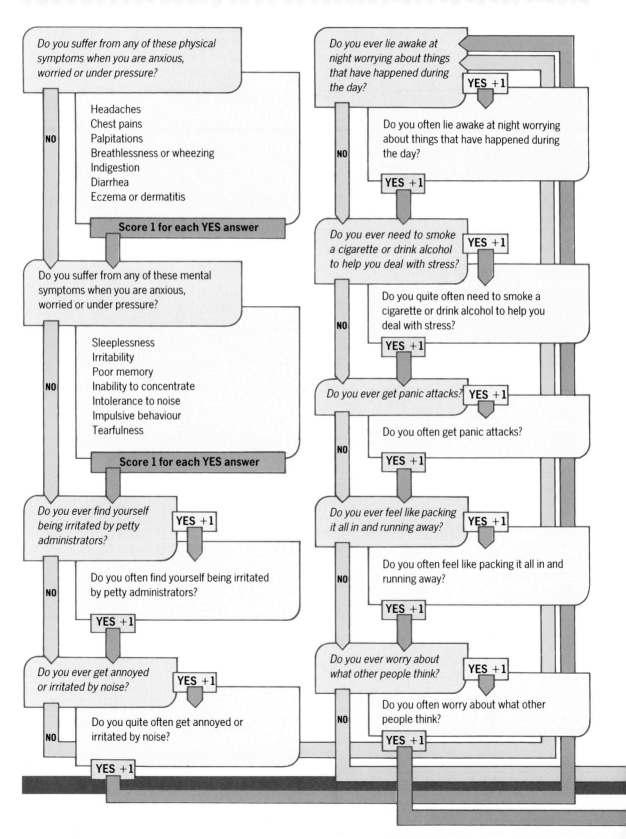

Do you suffer from any of these physical symptoms when you are anxious, worried or under pressure?

NO

Headaches
Chest pains
Palpitations
Breathlessness or wheezing
Indigestion
Diarrhea
Eczema or dermatitis

Score 1 for each YES answer

Do you suffer from any of these mental symptoms when you are anxious, worried or under pressure?

NO

Sleeplessness
Irritability
Poor memory
Inability to concentrate
Intolerance to noise
Impulsive behaviour
Tearfulness

Score 1 for each YES answer

Do you ever find yourself being irritated by petty administrators?   YES +1

NO   Do you often find yourself being irritated by petty administrators?

YES +1

Do you ever get annoyed or irritated by noise?   YES +1

NO   Do you quite often get annoyed or irritated by noise?

YES +1

Do you ever lie awake at night worrying about things that have happened during the day?   YES +1

NO   Do you often lie awake at night worrying about things that have happened during the day?

YES +1

Do you ever need to smoke a cigarette or drink alcohol to help you deal with stress?   YES +1

NO   Do you quite often need to smoke a cigarette or drink alcohol to help you deal with stress?

YES +1

Do you ever get panic attacks?   YES +1

NO   Do you often get panic attacks?

YES +1

Do you ever feel like packing it all in and running away?   YES +1

NO   Do you often feel like packing it all in and running away?

YES +1

Do you ever worry about what other people think?   YES +1

NO   Do you often worry about what other people think?

YES +1

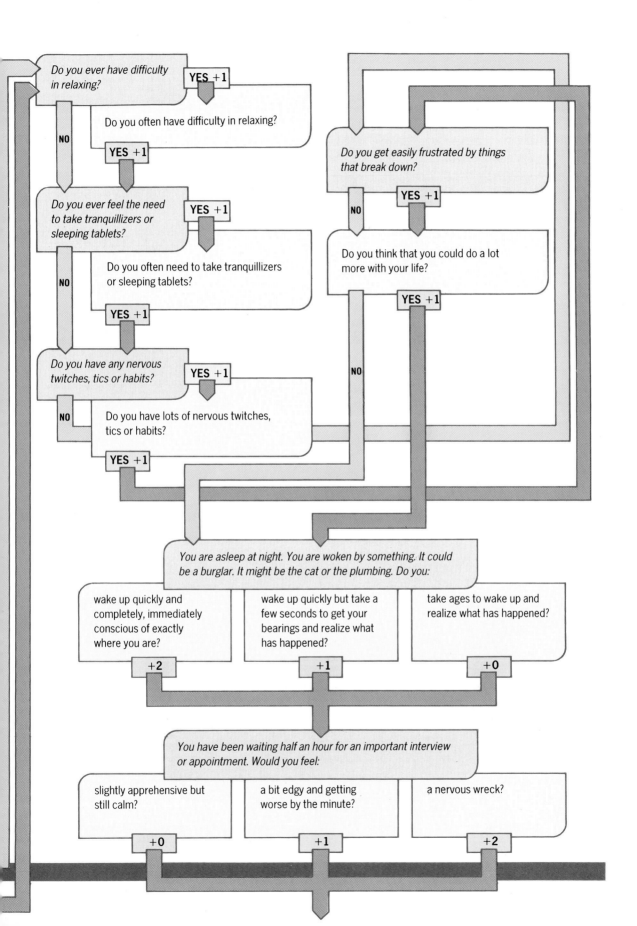

Do you ever have difficulty in relaxing? **YES +1**

Do you often have difficulty in relaxing? **YES +1**

NO

Do you get easily frustrated by things that break down? **YES +1**

NO

Do you ever feel the need to take tranquillizers or sleeping tablets? **YES +1**

Do you often need to take tranquillizers or sleeping tablets? **YES +1**

NO

Do you think that you could do a lot more with your life? **YES +1**

NO

Do you have any nervous twitches, tics or habits? **YES +1**

Do you have lots of nervous twitches, tics or habits? **YES +1**

NO

You are asleep at night. You are woken by something. It could be a burglar. It might be the cat or the plumbing. Do you:

wake up quickly and completely, immediately conscious of exactly where you are?	wake up quickly but take a few seconds to get your bearings and realize what has happened?	take ages to wake up and realize what has happened?
+2	+1	+0

You have been waiting half an hour for an important interview or appointment. Would you feel:

slightly apprehensive but still calm?	a bit edgy and getting worse by the minute?	a nervous wreck?
+0	+1	+2

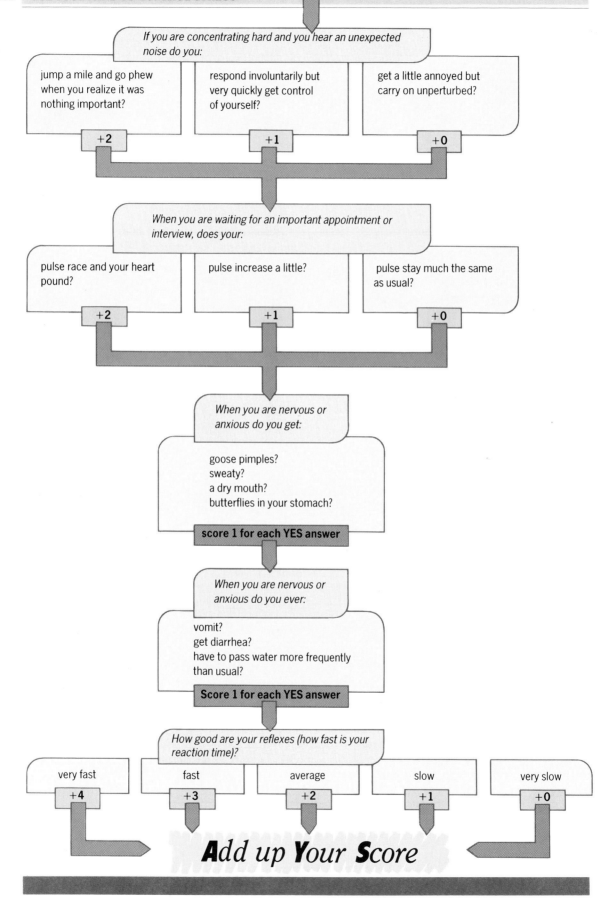

If you are concentrating hard and you hear an unexpected noise do you:

jump a mile and go phew when you realize it was nothing important?

+2

respond involuntarily but very quickly get control of yourself?

+1

get a little annoyed but carry on unperturbed?

+0

When you are waiting for an important appointment or interview, does your:

pulse race and your heart pound?

+2

pulse increase a little?

+1

pulse stay much the same as usual?

+0

When you are nervous or anxious do you get:

goose pimples?
sweaty?
a dry mouth?
butterflies in your stomach?

score 1 for each YES answer

When you are nervous or anxious do you ever:

vomit?
get diarrhea?
have to pass water more frequently than usual?

Score 1 for each YES answer

How good are your reflexes (how fast is your reaction time)?

very fast	fast	average	slow	very slow
+4	+3	+2	+1	+0

Add up **Y**our **S**core

*C*heck *Y*our *C*alculations

To find out whether stress is likely to harm your health, multiply the score you obtained in Part One of this flow chart by the score you obtained in Part Two. Your score for Part One should be between nought and 30, and for Part Two should be between nought and 55. Your total score will, therefore, be somewhere between nought and 1,650 (the maximum score being 30 × 55).

The higher your score, the more stress is affecting – or is likely to affect – your physical and mental health. Moreover, the higher your score, the more you need to learn how to control your exposure to stress and improve your resistance to stress-induced damage.

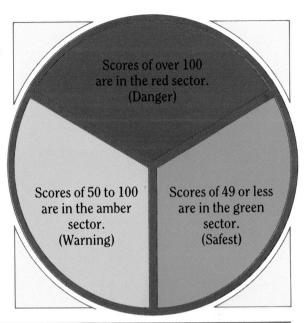

Scores of over 100 are in the red sector. (Danger)

Scores of 50 to 100 are in the amber sector. (Warning)

Scores of 49 or less are in the green sector. (Safest)

*H*ow to *R*educe the *D*amage done to you by *S*tress

If stress is harming your health – and your responses to stress are threatening your life – read the advice below, and try to follow it.

*T*he *T*en *P*oint *S*tress *C*ontrol *P*lan

 Learn how to relax. Read the advice in Chapter 4 and master the art of daydreaming.

 Write a list of all the things that are causing you stress. Then look through your list. Just writing down problems helps to make them less threatening, and having written them down, solutions often appear more readily. Tick off each problem as you solve it. You will be surprised to find that some problems will have sorted themselves out long before you have got round to ticking them off.

 Try to reduce your exposure to stress. For example, if you have a stressful job and you fill your relaxation hours with stressful activities, try to replace your current hobbies with relaxing, peaceful ones. If you are on too many committees or if you always play sports to win, try to disentangle yourself from such commitments.

 Do not be afraid to complain. If the politicians want to build a nuclear reactor in your back garden, do not sit back angrily. Write to your local newspaper, start a petition, let your feelings be known. Complaining may not always get the results you want, but it will help to minimize the feelings of frustration that can cause so much damage.

Yoga postures help to induce a state of profound relaxation of body and mind.

Learn how to deal with panic attacks. The ordinary symptoms associated with anxiety (butterflies in the stomach, diarrhea, headaches etc) are bad enough but, occasionally, these symptoms can build up into a panic attack. If you get such an attack, take a huge breath. Count up to four as you breathe in, hold your breath for a count of two. Then breathe out again, counting up to four, and hold your lungs empty for a count of two. Then do the whole thing again. Continue these simple breathing exercises for as long as you can.

Buy yourself a rocking chair. The rhythmic motion of a rocking chair helps to counteract urgent stress-related messages sent out by the brain. The rocking chair is a wooden tranquillizer that can help to relax your body and brain and drain away accumulated tensions.

Whenever you feel that the stress in your life has reached intolerable levels, go somewhere to unwind. If you have young children, try to leave them with friends for a few days. They will probably benefit if you can go away and come back relaxed. You could perhaps fix up a reciprocal arrangement with another couple. You can look after their children while they have a break and they can look after your children while you have a break. When you go away, do try to go somewhere peaceful and relaxing. Do not try to pack a lifetime's sightseeing into five days or else you will return home needing another holiday.

Try to share your problems with others who have the same difficulties. Whatever your problem may be – personal, social or financial – there are almost certainly many other people with similar problems. Visit your local library and community centre and find the names and addresses of local groups representing people who are likely to be able to help you with support and advice.

If you are planning a special event – such as a large party, a celebration or a house move – keep a special master plan to help you keep things running smoothly. List everything that has to be done and then mark off the dates by which time each problem must be solved. This will help you to keep unexpected disasters to an absolute minimum!

Minor frustrations produce a great deal of stress, so learn to cope with minor household problems yourself. It is becoming more and more difficult to get hold of repairmen. If you can deal with minor problems (including minor illnesses) yourself then you will be more independent.

7

Use Your Mind to Control Pain

People visiting patients in hospital have a far greater responsibility than they usually realize. If a visitor arrives looking and feeling miserable and then proceeds to bore the patient with a dreary account of an apparently endless series of local misfortunes ('Young Michael Roberts was killed in a motorbike crash', 'Mrs Nebworth has had another one of her funny turns', 'There was a gas leak at number 45', 'We lost 12 tiles in the storm the other night and the bedroom ceiling came down') the patient will probably feel considerably worse after his visitor has gone than he did before his visitor arrived!

On the other hand, if a visitor arrives with a couple of funny books, a magazine, a bunch of flowers and a host of amusing anecdotes, the patient will benefit enormously from the visit. He will get better quicker, will suffer less from pain and need fewer painkillers. Medical researchers have shown that cheerful visitors can have a dramatic influence on the health of people who are ill.

For some time, evidence has been available which shows that, by thinking about miserable, unhappy things, people can make themselves ill or make existing pains worse. However, in the last few years, experiments have been done which have shown that the human imagination can also have a very positive effect on pain. By learning to use your mind – and your imagination – you can get rid of pain very effectively. Of course, although visitors can help cheer up patients, they are not essential – patients can cheer up themselves! The following are just a few of the experiments which have shown that the imagination can have a powerful effect on the way that pain is perceived.

In 1974, John Horan and John Dellinger of Pennsylvania State University conducted a two-part experiment. In the first part of the experiment they instructed 36 volunteers to place their right hands in icy water and to keep them there for as long as they possibly could. If you think this sounds easy, just try it! After a few seconds, holding your hand in ice-cold water becomes a painful experience, and your hand will quickly let your brain know.

In the second part of the experiment, the researchers again asked their volunteers to keep their hands in icy water but, this time, the volunteers were told to try and imagine pleasant scenes. They were told to try to imagine that, instead of sitting in a laboratory with one hand in freezing cold water, they were sitting in a beautiful, peaceful place overlooking a wide, blue lake; or that they were walking through a lush, green meadow (these are the sort of daydreams that I have described on pages 92 to 100).

The results were very impressive. In the first part of the experiment, the male volunteers managed to keep their hands in iced water for an average of 69 seconds. The women volunteers managed to keep their hands in the water for an average of 34 seconds. In the second part of the experiment, when they were encouraged to use their imaginations to enable them to keep their hands in the icy water for as long as possible, the men managed an average of 117 seconds and the women an average of 176 seconds. As many other experiments have confirmed, women tend to respond much more readily to their imaginations than men. Men seem

more inclined to regard the whole idea as rather silly and preposterous.

In 1977, Donald Scott and Theodore Barber from Massachusetts paid 80 undergraduates from Boston $3 each to stick their hands in icy water. In the first stage of the experiment, members of a control group were told simply to keep their hands in the iced water for as long as possible. In the second part of the experiment the students were told:

'There are two ways that you can react to this test. One way is to get all fussed up and bothered about the sensations. The other way is to use some strategies that will affect your perception of pain and your ability to tolerate it. One strategy you can use while your hand is in the apparatus is to concentrate on other things during this time. Another strategy you can use is to become aware of the sensations, but do not think of them as painful but as unusual. A related way is to think of your hand as a wax or rubber hand and not really part of you. A final strategy you can use when sensations level off is to think as if your hand feels dull and insensitive.'

Once again the results were very impressive. The volunteers who were merely told to try to hold their hands in icy water for as long as possible managed an average of 279 seconds, while those who were given the alternative strategies for dealing with pain managed an average of 435 seconds. (The fact that this group managed to keep their hands in the cold water for much longer than the group of volunteers used by Horan and Dellinger is not significant – the water could have been warmer. What is important is the *improvement* that was recorded in both experiments when the power of the mind over the body was employed.)

In 1978, Matt Jaremko from the University of Richmond, Virginia, conducted another experiment which proved the same point. Jaremko told his volunteers to imagine that they were in a desert on a hot day and that they were feeling uncomfortably tired. He told them to think of the icy water into which they were plunging their hands as cool and refreshing! Jaremko concluded that the technique worked very well, especially for subjects who used their imaginations powerfully. He concluded: 'The extent to which a person gets involved in imagining the strategies has an influence on the effect of changing pain tolerance. Those who are highly involved show a pronounced enhancement effect.'

Many more researchers have produced similar results. Dr Lorne Hartman, Director of the Behavior Therapy Program at the Clarke Institute of Psychiatry in Toronto, and Kenneth Ainsworth, Psychometrist in the Department of Psychology at Chedoke Hospital in Hamilton, Ontario, published a report in 1980 which showed that, by using their imaginations to picture peaceful images, patients could successfully control their pain. Michael Rosenbaum from Haifa University in Israel has obtained similar results.

The conclusion to be drawn from all this research has to be that pain can be controlled with the aid of the imagination. Many scientists and doctors who have received an orthodox medical training still find this sort of evidence difficult to accept. Ever since men first started to practise medicine, it has been generally accepted that relief can only be obtained by using some outside aid – usually a herb or a pill of some kind. Doctors trained in the traditional way find it difficult to accept that the powers of the human mind can be so complete. Yet the results of the research are indisputable. There is no longer any scientific doubt about it: we can use our imaginations to help us increase our ability to withstand pain and to help us control it without using drugs.

How to Measure Pain

If you are going to prove to yourself that you are successfully learning to control your pain, you must be able to measure it – which is not easy. It is, of course, impossible to measure pain objectively. You cannot compare the pain you get in your back with the pain your neighbour gets in her leg. Likewise it is quite impossible for you to measure the pains that you get in your head with the pains your father gets in his chest.

However, you can measure *variation* in one particular pain, and you can tell if a *specific* pain of yours is getting better or worse by the way in which you describe it to yourself. That can be extremely useful because if you can measure your pain, you can judge the effectiveness of the technique you are using to control it.

Pain Measurement – technique 1

Look through the following list of words and pick out the four which you think describe your pain most accurately. Remember you can only choose FOUR words. Once you have picked out your four words, add up the numbers beside the words you have chosen. The total will give you your 'Current Pain Score'.

When you want to see if your pain is getting better or worse, merely repeat the exercise. Look through the list again and pick another four words. Add up your score and compare it with your previous score. You can keep a record of your scores over the coming months to find out how effectively you are controlling your pain.

Sore (1)	Tingling (1)	Intense (3)	Murderous (4)
Dull (1)	Disagreeable (1)	Horrible (3)	Vicious (4)
Tender (1)	Unpleasant (1)	Fierce (3)	Intolerable (4)
Uncomfortable (1)	Stinging (1)	Agonizing (3)	Maddening (4)
Annoying (1)	Tiring (2)	Exhausting (3)	Killing (4)
Troublesome (1)	Heavy (2)	Burning (3)	Paralysing (4)
Throbbing (1)	Sickening (2)	Frightful (3)	Excruciating (4)
Smarting (1)	Miserable (2)	Wretched (3)	Unbearable (4)
Aching (1)	Distressing (2)	Punishing (3)	Terrifying (4)

Pain Measurement – technique 2

Record your pain level according to the chart below – making a note of the time and of whatever pain-relieving technique you may have used. Then compare the level of your pain on subsequent occasions.

0	No pain	0
½		½
1	Mild pain	1
1½		1½
2	Moderate pain	2
2½		2½
3	Severe pain	3
3½		3½
4	Intolerable pain	4
4½		4½

How do you Respond to Pain – and how can you Improve your Resistance to Pain?

Next time there is an athletics race on television, take a careful look at the athletes at the end. The winner will look fit and fresh. He will probably carry on running around the track to receive the applause of the crowd. But the runners who came second and third will be standing with their hands on their knees, gasping for breath and in obvious discomfort. Is the winner always that much better than the rest of the field? Of course he is not!

You can see exactly the same thing happening in all other sports, too. Next time there is a boxing match on television, take a look at the two fighters when the bout comes to an end and the winner has been announced. At the final bell, both fighters might have looked tired but determined. After the announcement, the victor will look fresh and lively and the loser will look exhausted and weary. He will *look* defeated!

The same thing happens to two football teams, or two teams of oarsmen. Just look around and you will find that it is not at all difficult to find dozens of practical examples of the way that an individual's mental state affects the way that he feels or responds to pain.

Pain is often made worse by fear, anxiety and disappointment. If you can relax yourself, cheer yourself up, calm yourself and generally keep yourself amused, your pain – no matter what has caused it – will be less destructive.

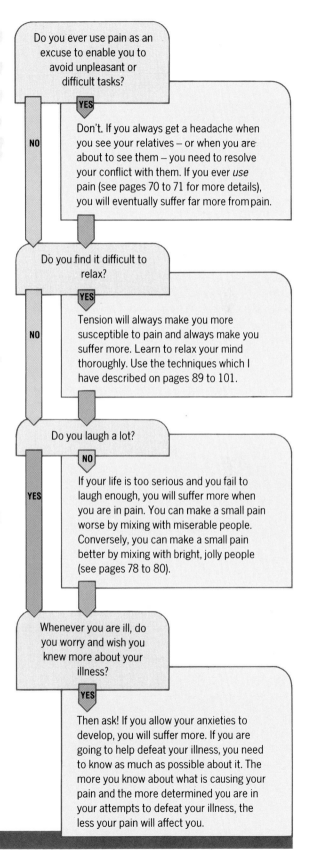

Do you ever use pain as an excuse to enable you to avoid unpleasant or difficult tasks?

YES

Don't. If you always get a headache when you see your relatives – or when you are about to see them – you need to resolve your conflict with them. If you ever *use* pain (see pages 70 to 71 for more details), you will eventually suffer far more from pain.

NO

Do you find it difficult to relax?

YES

Tension will always make you more susceptible to pain and always make you suffer more. Learn to relax your mind thoroughly. Use the techniques which I have described on pages 89 to 101.

NO

Do you laugh a lot?

NO

If your life is too serious and you fail to laugh enough, you will suffer more when you are in pain. You can make a small pain worse by mixing with miserable people. Conversely, you can make a small pain better by mixing with bright, jolly people (see pages 78 to 80).

YES

Whenever you are ill, do you worry and wish you knew more about your illness?

YES

Then ask! If you allow your anxieties to develop, you will suffer more. If you are going to help defeat your illness, you need to know as much as possible about it. The more you know about what is causing your pain and the more determined you are in your attempts to defeat your illness, the less your pain will affect you.

Ways to Conquer Pain

By regarding your pain as an enemy and by developing a range of imaginative combative skills, you can take an active part in controlling it. You can use your imagination in a positive, constructive and powerful way. Here are some pain-controlling techniques that you can try. Remember that you will benefit most if you develop and use your own images. Use the techniques I have described as blueprints for your own methods of pain control. Some of the techniques described here depend on the principle of creative visualization – you will find more background information about this in the following chapter.

These techniques are powerful. Check with your doctor first if you are going to try any of them. Pain is an important protective mechanism and there are times when you must be careful about overcoming or ignoring it. Remember, too, that you should not use these techniques when driving a car or operating dangerous machinery.

Imagine that you have left your body and that you are watching yourself from the other side of the room. Try to 'see' yourself as though you were a ghost in the corner or a fly on the wall. To begin with, you can see that you are in considerable pain. Then, while you watch yourself, you see a young nurse approach. She is gentle, sympathetic and kind. She holds your hand and caresses your brow. She is then joined by a second nurse. Both nurses are loving, compassionate, gentle people. They want to help you. They want to help ease your pain. As you watch, you see yourself gradually looking more and more comfortable. When you feel the pain is under control, you can return to your body.

Try to alter the context in which your pain has appeared. For example, if you are sitting in the dentist's chair and the dentist is about to attack your teeth with his drill, imagine for a moment that he is a ruthless and cruel KGB interrogator. Imagine that you are a spy and that you are trying hard to protect your 'cell'. Imagine that every move the dentist makes is designed to help him get information from you. Make up your mind that he will not succeed. Afterwards, you may have to explain to the dentist why you snarled at him, but he will understand!

You can use this technique in all sorts of ways. If you have painful, arthritic feet and you are determined to force yourself to walk, imagine that you are a fighter pilot and that you have parachuted out over enemy territory. Imagine that you have injured your feet, ankles or legs, but that you must get back through enemy lines as soon as possible. If you have arthritic hands, imagine that you are a concert pianist who loves to perform and that you must get the movement back into your wrists and fingers in order to play at an important concert. By creating a powerful, imaginary scene for yourself, you will increase your ability to cope with pain, disability and discomfort. Your mind will help you overcome the weaknesses of your body.

Take yourself off to a relaxing, calming place where you can rest quietly and get away from your immediate surroundings and from cares and concerns. You can, if you like, use some of the daydreaming techniques which I described on pages 92 to 101. Make up daydreaming scenes of your own as well.

Try to dominate your pain by concentrating on specific mental problems. Give yourself word or number games to play. Set yourself mental arithmetic exercises. Play word games which mean that you have to try and think of words – and then remember them. For example, try to think of six-letter words beginning with each letter of the alphabet in turn. When you have done that, try to think of four-letter words, five-letter words and so on. See what you score out of a possible top score of 26.

Imagine that pain is being transmitted around your body through a series of thin wires. Try to see the wires connecting the parts of your body to your brain. Imagine that deep inside your body there is an army of tiny surgeons, and each surgeon is equipped with a pair of wire cutters. Now send your team of surgeons around your body to cut the pain-carrying wires. Make sure that they concentrate *only* on the areas where the pain is most severe. Imagine that, as each wire is cut, you feel relief from pain.

Try to see the pain in your body as a small, invading army of very dirty, grubby, grey cells. Imagine that all the pain in your body is produced by these nasty cells. Imagine that the grubby, grey cells are laughing at you and enjoying your discomfort. They want to cause you more discomfort. They enjoy seeing you miserable. Now try to imagine that your body has a fine force of good, white cells that can overcome and defeat the grey, pain-producing cells. Send your force of painkilling cells out around your body to attack the invaders. Envisage the white cells fighting and destroying the grey cells. Imagine that your body's own fighting force is defeating the cells that are causing your pain.

Use your brain's creative powers to overwhelm the pain messages. Try to write songs or create limericks. Try to remember the names of all your friends. Try to remember all the people you have ever met. Try to remember all the people you have kissed. Try working out chess problems without a board. Give a lecture about something you are interested in to a huge, imaginary hall full of people. Think of something sexy – create a fantasy that will help you to forget reality for a few moments. In a sexual fantasy there are no limits; you can allow yourself to behave freely and irresponsibly, responding only to your whims and fancies. It does not matter how you use your brain's creative powers, the important thing is to find something to capture your imagination and your enthusiasm.

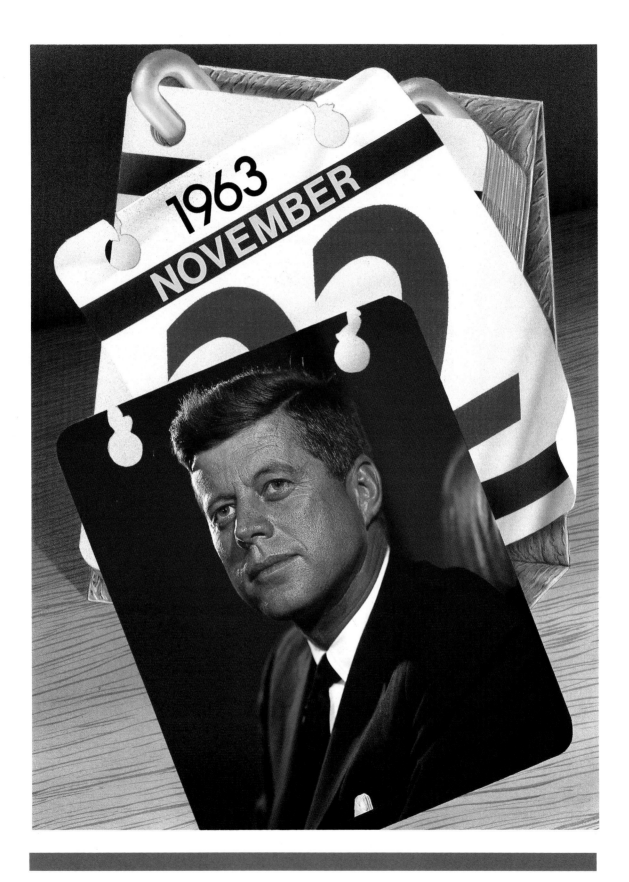

8

ind orkout

Many people remember what they were doing at significant dates – such as the day Kennedy was assassinated. To improve your memory, try to be aware of each day in your life as special, memorable and important. (See page 138).

The more you learn how to use your mind and your imagination, the more you will benefit, not just by having better health but also by having greater powers of memory and concentration. Most of us under-use our mental powers.

Shakespeare understood the power of the human mind. He wrote that 'There is nothing good or bad but thinking makes it so'. More recently the philosopher William James announced that, in his opinion, human beings could, by changing the inner attitudes of their minds, change the outer aspects of their lives, and thereby control their own destinies. Shakespeare was writing 400 years ago, James a century ago.

Only in the last few years have these philosophical conclusions been translated into practical reality. While the majority of doctors around the world have continued to use knives, poisons, chemicals, radiation and electricity to attack disease and disorder (using the human body as a battleground and sometimes forgetting that, in a battle, the battleground can often be as badly damaged as the opponent), a small but impressive group of researchers has continued to explore the power of the human imagination. They have shown that, used wisely, the imagination can be a simple, but sophisticated, weapon, remarkably easy to use, free of side-effects and far more powerful than any other tool ever investigated.

As I have already shown in the introduction, if a man thinks that he is going to die, the chances are that he will die. If a woman thinks, and really believes, that she is going to develop cancer, she probably will. If a woman thinks she is going to get pregnant, she probably will get pregnant. If a man expects an accident, he is bound to have one.

It is the raw and impressive power of the imagination over the body that explains the strengths and skills of the African witchdoctor. It is this very same power that so many patients respond to positively when they are given pills that contain nothing but sugar. It is also this power that explains how untrained healers can so often conquer pain and disease with their bare hands.

In the past, the powers of the mind were used most dramatically by interventionists wanting to take advantage of these natural skills in all of us to augment their own powers. Homeopaths, hypnotherapists, acupuncturists and orthodox practitioners of all kinds have used the patient's imagination to help them obtain a cure. When the professional suggests to a patient that a certain treatment will help him, the patient's imagination is brought into action. Inevitably, when a cure occurs, the professional takes the credit. But you do not need to visit a professional health expert or healer in order to take advantage of the powers of your mind. You need only believe in the power of your mind.

Creative visualization, or the use of mental imagery, is one of the simplest and most powerful ways in which you can use your mind to help preserve your health. In the previous chapter dealing with pain, I explained some simple mental imagery exercises on page 127. But let us start right at the beginning.

Try to remember when you last had an ordinary, common cold. Now try to imagine how you would feel today if you felt the first symptoms of a cold developing – the sore throat, the slight headache, the beginnings of a cough, the stuffed-up nose and so on. If you respond to those early symptoms by seeing yourself snuffling in bed and missing all your

Alternative medicine offers natural remedies that assist your body to good health without recourse to drugs.

important – and perhaps stressful – appointments for a week, the chances are that you *will* end up in bed, feeling terrible and missing all sorts of very important appointments. Your cold will have a very bad effect on your life. If, however, when your first cold symptoms develop, you visualize yourself getting better within a few hours and confronting your responsibilities with vigour, your symptoms will probably disappear quite soon and you will not need to miss any appointments.

Let me tell you a personal anecdote that illustrates exactly what I mean. A couple of years ago, I was getting towards the end of a book promotional tour that had gone on and on. In the space of two weeks I had visited dozens of television and radio studios and I had talked to heaven knows how many newspaper and magazine reporters. I was absolutely shattered. I had covered hundreds of miles by train, car, aeroplane and on foot. I had answered the same questions a thousand times.

With less than a week of the tour to go, I woke up with the first signs of a terrible cold. My head ached and my throat was sore. My legs, arms and back felt as though I had just run a marathon in lead boots. I had the first signs of 'flu. I still had several important interviews to do and I knew that if I could keep going, it would help the book a great deal. I also knew that if I could just get through the next few days, I could take a proper rest for a week or so.

Feeling rather foolish, I lay in my bed and made a deal with my body – and with the cold bug I had acquired. I told them both that I needed another five days of good health and that I could not spare the time to be ill. I explained that I would put up with the cold symptoms when the book promotional tour was over. Then I got up, had a shower, dressed and carried on with my tour. My nose was unblocked, my throat felt fine and my muscles felt strong.

I got through the rest of the promotional tour without any physical discomfort. Everything went well, and the book sold out and had to be reprinted quickly. When the tour was over, I went back home. I had completely forgotten about the deal I had made with my body, but my body had not. I had hardly taken off my shoes on the last day of my tour before the symptoms of that cold returned. Once again I had a sore throat, a bad head, a developing cough and a stuffed-up nose. I had all the symptoms that I had had five days earlier.

That was the first time that I realized that the human mind has enormous, and usually untapped, powers. I have told that anecdote because I hope that it illustrates well the way in which the power of the mind can operate. But the anecdote does not even begin to show the extent of the mind's power.

You can use your imagination to control your body – and your health – in exactly the same way. With a little practice and enthusiasm, you can use your imagination to help you combat far more serious threats – and combat them not temporarily, but permanently. The first and, perhaps, the most important thing to remember whenever you fall ill is that you should always think of your body as being powerful and strong and of any disease or infection as being weak. We tend to be frightened of words like 'cancer' because we think that cancer is a powerful and dangerous disease. Do not let cancer start with an advantage like that.

If you have an infection of any kind, think of the organism causing it as being evil but dreadfully weak, lonely and frightened. Think of it as being a long way from home and very nervous; and regard your body as a real tower of strength. If you have a cancer, view it as an uncertain, unsettled intruder. If you think of your cancer as an entity, then think of it as weak and weedy, having terrible skin and an awful cough.

With this background, you can then build up your ability to use your imagination. For example, if you are suffering from an infection and you are being treated with drugs, imagine that each tablet or capsule is filled with special, miniature fighting forces. Imagine those forces being released in your stomach, finding their way around your bloodstream and then attacking the disease that has had the temerity to attack you. Imagine the white blood cells in your body as a tough, fighting force struggling to repel attackers and invaders. Think of your body's defences as Knights of the Round Table fighting bad knights, or as cowboys fighting Indians, or as the cavalry, or as spacemen attacking invaders from another planet.

To see some other ways in which you can use your mind to help your body, turn back to pages 128 to 129, where I have explained exactly how you can use your imagination to help overcome pain.

Before I leave the subject of creative visualization, I want to explain how you can use this sort of skill to help improve your sporting skills. At the start of this book, on pages 24 to 26, I explained how sports stars like Arthur Ashe and Dennis Connor have used their minds to help them win. Now, I want briefly to explain to you how you can train your mind to help you improve your sporting ability.

It has been known for many years that the mind can have a dramatic influence on any sportsman's prowess. It is, for example, well accepted that when a football team plays a match on its home turf it has a real advantage over its opponents. Why should this be? The size of the pitch has not changed, the rules have not changed. Yet a team playing a home

---

The trick is to envisage yourself winning. You cannot, of course, turn yourself into a world champion simply by using your imagination, but you can improve your game – whatever you play – and you can maximize your chances of winning every time you play. Here are some tricks that will help you.

Once in every game, you will probably play a shot of which you are really proud. A tennis player will serve an ace. A golfer will play a magnificent bunker shot that ends up within a foot of the pin. Every time you do this, savour the moment. Try to remember exactly how you felt as you played the shot. Remember what the conditions were. Recall the temperature, your surroundings, the smells and so on. If you can play that shot once, you can play it again and again and again. However, to be able to benefit from that single experience, you must be able to remember how you played the shot the first time.

Practise as much as you can and try to acquire a number of muscle movements and reflex actions. Every time you play a good practice shot, try to remember it. Every time you play a bad practice shot, make sure you forget it.

match acknowledges that it has the edge over the visiting side. Even when a visiting side brings its supporters with it, the home team still has an advantage.

The reason for this is that the team members who are playing at home are playing on a pitch where they have practised and where they can easily remember many of the things they have been taught. With a little luck, they will also be able to remember their previous successes. If the team manager is a skilled psychologist, the dressing room will contain a list of previous victories. Cups and trophies won by the team will be conspicuously displayed.

If the coach understands the power of the mind, he will have made sure that the majority of the team's coaching and training sessions took place on the pitch where the big matches will be played. He will know that, just as students do better when they take their examinations in a room where they have been taught, so sportsmen do better on a pitch or ground where they have learnt their skills and experienced triumphs.

What is true for a team player is, of course, also true for a player who works alone, like a golfer. The golfer who plays a big tournament on his home course, where he can remember the good shots he has made and where he has been taught many of his skills, will usually do better than when he plays on a strange course that he has not visited before.

So far, I have dealt with a factor over which few of us have much, if any, influence: the ground where we play a match. However, there is much that any sportsperson can do to improve his game, wherever he may be playing. By using his imagination and by using the power of his mind, the sportsperson can greatly increase his chances of doing well.

The first and most important point is that the sportsman or sportswoman must have confidence. The golfer who thinks, 'I always miss shots like this,' probably will miss it. The pool player who thinks a shot is impossible will almost certainly miss it. The tennis player who does not think he or she will win a particular point will almost certainly lose it.

Next time you are playing in an important match, try to switch yourself in to automatic. You need to let your reflexes take over and set aside your fears if you are to play a perfect, natural game and avoid the danger of succumbing to nerves on the big occasion.

Each time you are about to play a shot, use your memories from the past. Try to recall the last time you played such a shot and got it absolutely right. Try to use your imagination so that you re-enact the muscular movements which enabled you to play that shot so perfectly before. Let your imagination set and control your muscles. Let your memory take over and smother pessimism and anxiety with real confidence. Try to see yourself playing the perfect shot and never visualize yourself playing a bad shot. Always see yourself playing every aspect of the shot as perfectly as possible.

*R*edefining the *P*ast

A woman telephoned me on a radio phone-in programme not long ago and wanted to know if I could help her eradicate an extremely unpleasant memory that was, she told me, ruining her life.

'It happened about two years ago', she said. 'I was in the house on my own one afternoon when two men broke in. They were both wearing masks. They tied me up to a chair in the kitchen, threatened me with a knife and stole my purse and some money I'd got hidden in a drawer.'

'Did they hurt you?' I asked her.

'No,' said the woman, quietly.

'They didn't assault you sexually?'

'No.'

'Tell me how what happened then is affecting you now,' I asked her.

There was a silence while the woman thought for a few moments. 'It's difficult to explain,' she said at last. 'But I still have difficulty in going to sleep at night and I don't like being left alone in the house.'

'Do you think the two men will come back again?' I asked her.

'I don't think so,' said the woman. 'I didn't have much money then and I haven't got much money now. I wouldn't have thought they'd think it worth their while robbing me again.'

'What can you remember about the men?' I asked her.

'Not much,' said the woman. 'They kept their masks on all the time.'

'How big were they?'

'Quite big,' said the woman.

'Think hard,' I said. 'Really hard. Try to remember exactly how big they were.'

'They were both medium height, I suppose,' said the woman. 'They weren't all that big.'

'And how old do you think they were?'

'I don't think they were more than about 17 or 18,' the woman told me. 'That's what I told the police.'

'The police didn't ever catch them?'

'No,' said the woman.

'When you have difficulty in getting to sleep what do you think of?' I asked the caller.

'I think about the two men breaking in,' said the woman. 'I just keep re-living it.'

'When you re-live your experience, do you think you see that dreadful experience the way it really happened?' I asked. 'Think very carefully before you answer.'

There was a much longer pause. 'No, I suppose not,' admitted the woman.

'What's the difference?'

'When I re-live it they're much bigger and tougher and nastier,' the woman told me eventually. 'It was a terrible experience but over the years I think it's got worse. Sometimes I have nightmares about it and then there are often a dozen of them. In my nightmares, they are huge and they all have knives and chains and they are very menacing.'

'How much did they steal from you?'

'I had a few pounds in my purse and another £10 or £15 hidden,' the woman told me.

'Let's look at the facts,' I suggested. 'Two teenagers put masks on, broke into your house and stole a total of about £20 from you. Is that a fair summary?'

'Yes,' said the woman, 'It doesn't sound so bad when you say it like that, does it?'

'I'm not trying to belittle your experience,' I told her. 'It was undoubtedly an awful thing to happen. But if you're going to overcome it you've got to be able to put it into perspective.' The woman said nothing. I suspect that she nodded at the other end of the telephone line. 'They sound like a fairly sorry pair of crooks,' I said. 'Don't you think?'

She laughed nervously. 'It was hardly the Great Train Robbery, was it?'

'They sound as if they were a pair of bungling, inept amateurs,' I said. 'Maybe just a couple of kids who were out of work and looking for a few quid. Would you agree?'

'Yes, I think so,' said the woman. 'I certainly don't think they were professionals. They didn't even take our TV set or video. The police were quite surprised about that.'

'Were they nervous when they were robbing you?' I asked.

'Pardon?' asked the woman, who was clearly confused by my question.

'Were they nervous?' I asked her. 'Did they seem edgy?'

'They were both sweating,' said the woman. 'I could smell the sweat on them. And one of them kept wiping his hands on his trousers. He was very nervous. He was the one who had the knife.'

'Do you think they were as nervous as you were?'

'Probably,' said the woman. There was a silence for a moment. 'I think they probably were just as nervous as I was,' she confessed.

'Are you beginning to see what happened to you in a different light yet?' I asked.

The woman agreed that she was. 'It all seems a bit daft, really,' she said with a nervous laugh.

'Do you still feel terrified of them?'

'If anything,' said the woman thoughtfully, 'I feel sorry for them.'

'Do you think you'll be able to live more easily with the memory of it?' I asked the woman.

'Oh yes,' she said. 'Yes, I do.'

I have described that conversation at some length because I think it illustrates very well just how we can exaggerate and distort things in our own minds and how we can magnify events when we look back at them. Our minds have a tendency to exaggerate and to make things seem much worse than they really were. If there is a memory which worries or upsets you, try to put it into perspective. Ask yourself the sorts of questions I asked that woman telephone caller. Try to see if your imagination has created a big problem out of a smaller one. The imagination can do you a good deal of harm. Redefining your memory can help you enormously.

The Kennedy Factor

What were you doing when the American President John F. Kennedy was assassinated? Can you remember? Most people can. Yet Kennedy was assassinated in November 1963. You may often complain that your memory is terrible and you may frequently wish that you could remember things better, but I suspect that it is not your memory that is at fault, but how you use it. Try answering the following questions:

What did you do last Christmas?

What were you doing when Prince Charles and Lady Diana Spencer got married? Where were you at the time of the wedding?

How did you spend your last birthday?

Have you ever had a car crash? If so, can you describe it? Can you describe what happened afterwards?

Can you remember your first real love affair? Can you remember falling in love for the first time? Can you remember the details of your first real kiss?

Can you remember what you were doing when you heard that Elvis Presley had died?

Can you remember what you were doing when you heard that John Lennon had been shot?

The chances are that, even though some of these events happened months or years ago, you can answer several of the questions fairly accurately. On each of those occasions you can probably remember what you were doing, who you were with, even the weather. Yet you probably say that you have a rotten memory. Indeed, you may have difficulty in remembering what you were doing last Tuesday. You would have to get out your old diaries to find out what you were doing on May 18 1981.

Why the difference? Why are our memories sometimes capable of quite remarkable feats and sometimes next to useless? The explanation is that most of the time we are only half awake, dead to the world around us. We do not see, hear or feel many of the things which are there to be perceived.

If you want to improve your memory – and be better aware of the things that are happening to you every day – read through and act upon the following advice.

 Try to be aware of each day in your life as special, memorable and important. Each morning, as you wake up, try to remember that you may be starting the most memorable day of your life. By doing this, you will increase the intensity with which you live.

 Increase your sensuous awareness of the world around you. Many of us eat wonderful food without tasting it, we drive past beautiful scenery without seeing it and we listen to magnificent music without hearing it. Make sure that you smell, taste, hear, see and feel everything in your life that is there to be smelt, tasted, heard, seen or felt.

 Do not let your dreams die. Remember the dreams you had when you were 17 or 18 years old. Your dreams may have been submerged in a world of drudgery and routine. Get them out and dust them off. Remember that it is never too late to recapture the excitements and the ambitions that you had when you were young. Look hard at what you do and at its significance. Try to eradicate meaningless and insignificant trivia from your life. Ask yourself why you do things. Remember that you only live once. Take a real interest in what you do. If you find your life dull and dreary, change things!

 Concentrate hard on everything you do. Work in short sharp bursts to keep your attention strong and to stop yourself getting bored. When you feel your attention wandering, switch to something else.

 Practise by working your way through the last 24 hours. Try to remember everything you have done and everything you have tasted, heard or seen.

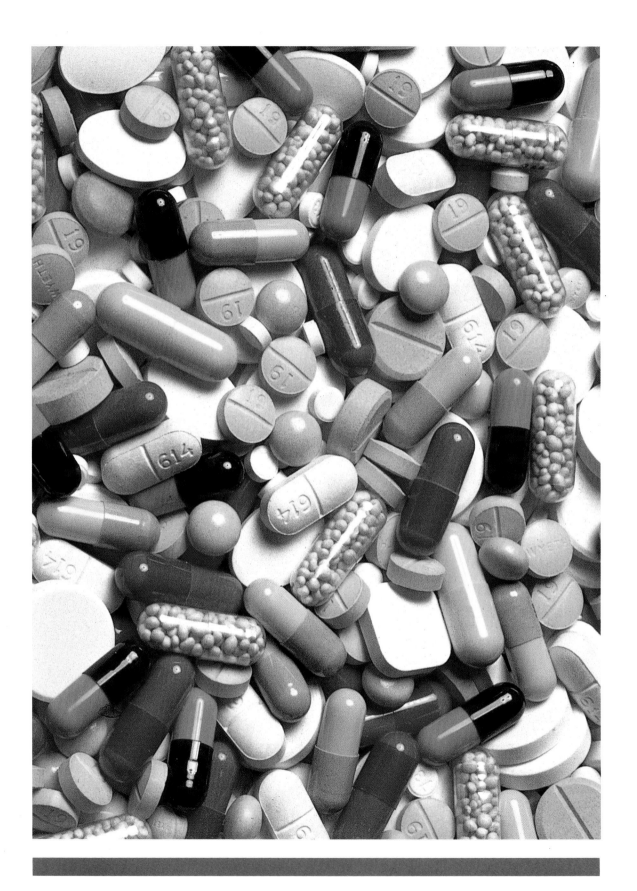

9
Be Your Own Doctor

Modern drug companies offer a bewildering array of capsules and pills to treat the multitude of ailments that beset modern man. In many cases there are easier and better ways of achieving good health.

When faced with a patient who has a specific disease, most doctors will still prefer to offer an interventionist therapy. They will prescribe a pill, suggest surgery or offer some other form of 'attacking' treatment. Most alternative practitioners favour a similar approach. If you go to see an acupuncturist and tell him that you are ill, he will want to stick needles in you. If you see a herbalist, he will want to give you a herbal medicine. If you visit a homoeopath, he will prescribe a homoeopathic medicine.

Few professional health workers will suggest that you try to heal yourself by your mind's power, or that you can assist their interventionist approach by using your imagination. Yet, as I have already shown, the evidence strongly suggests that in many cases you can treat yourself effectively and safely by using the power of your mind. And why not? Your mind has probably made you ill. Why should it not make you better?

I am not, of course, advocating that you ignore your doctor altogether. On some occasions they provide an essential, life-saving service. They can offer surgical remedies for problems which are not self limiting and they can offer nursing care and facilities for the disabled and the weak. You should, of course, consult your doctor about any symptoms which require diagnosis or medical attention and you should ask for his or her help if you are uncertain or worried in any way.

You should also, however, become aware of your body's recuperative powers. Learn to use those powers *and* learn to recognize when you are likely to need professional help. If and when you do need the help of a doctor, retain control of your body, bringing in your doctor as an adviser and technical consultant rather than as someone in sole charge.

If you have a headache and you visit your doctor then you will probably be given pills, which the doctor has been trained to provide. Having learned to use the power of your mind over your body you may well be able to treat your headache yourself, but should you fail you can still visit your doctor. The beauty of using the power of the mind is that you have everything to gain by it and nothing to lose. In this chapter, I am going to describe how you can use the power of your mind to help tackle a few, specific disorders. You will, I think, soon see how these techniques can be adapted to help combat a much wider range of conditions.

Asthma

Sleeplessness

Do you get as much love as you need?

NO

YES

Asthma sufferers often need more love than they usually receive, but may not *give* as much love as they should. Do you tell your loved ones how you feel every day? Do you kiss and hug the people you love every day? Maybe you would receive more love if you gave more!

Do you share your emotions with others?

NO

YES

Asthma sufferers often do not share feelings easily. If you are cross, sad or angry, let people know. If you feel happy, share your emotions. Do not hide tears or laughter.

Do you ever wheeze or suffer from a tight chest?

NO

YES

This is because the muscles of your chest constrict and stop air getting in and out of your lungs. You may be able to relieve your symptoms by imagining that you can see the constricted tubes within your lungs and then deliberately relaxing and opening those passageways. This really does work. After all, if stress can narrow the tubes in your lungs, why should relaxation not open them up again?

Do you have difficulty in relaxing at night?

YES

NO

Relax your body before getting into bed. Take a brisk walk for 15 minutes. Think through your day's problems. Write down all your worries in a notebook. Have a soothing, warm bath for another ten or 15 minutes. Allow your mind to float quite freely. If any fresh thoughts pop into your head, write them down. Go to bed with a relaxing book. This will help eradicate the day's problems from your head. As soon as you are ready for sleep, close your eyes and create for yourself a soothing, relaxing daydream. (See pages 92 to 101.)

YES

Do you ever lie awake thinking about the day's problems?

Can you relax?

NO

You should learn (see pages 89 to 101). Once you can relax properly, you will be able to prevent many asthma attacks and cure those that do occur.

*H*eart *D*isease

Do you push yourself too hard?

NO

YES

This is common among heart attack victims. Try to re-establish sensible priorities. Do you have enough time to rest and relax? Try to decide what you want out of life. Maybe you do not need to push so hard.

Can you relax?

YES

NO

Relaxation does not just mean flopping down in front of the television with a drink. You have to practise if you want to relax properly. (See pages 89 to 101).

Are you impatient and aggressive?

YES

Do not let your anger kill you (see page 75). Try to put problems into perspective. Decide whether a problem is worth getting excited about before getting excited. Write down problems that annoy you.

High Blood Pressure

Can you relax?

NO

Set aside ten or 20 minutes a day for relaxation. If you learn to relax properly, you may be able to control your blood pressure without pills.

YES

Do you have stormy relationships with others?

YES

So do many people with high blood pressure. Take a close look at all your relationships. Use the questions on pages 60 to 61 to help you.

NO

Are you unusually competitive and particularly aggressive?

YES

When you feel yourself becoming cross, ask yourself whether your anger is really justified. If it is, let it out. If not, forget it.

Eczema and Dermatitis

Do you hide your emotions?

YES

Eczema sufferers often do. Try to let your emotions out. Cry when you feel sad, laugh when you feel happy and bang your fist when you are angry!

NO

Do you lack confidence?

YES

Then build up your self-confidence. Write a TV advertisement for yourself. Make it exciting.

NO

Do you know how to relax?

NO

By learning how to relax (see pages 89 to 101), you will reduce the chances of your eczema developing and increase the chances of your being able to get rid of eczema if it has already developed.

*O*verweight

Do you let other people decide how much you will eat?

YES

You need to be more assertive. YOU should decide how much you eat, whether you have second helpings and when you stop eating. Just remember that it is the people who are insisting on your having a second helping who are behaving unreasonably. You have the right to say no to a forceful hostess.

NO

Do you feel defeatist at the prospect of starting a diet?

YES

Start with a short-term aim. You need an attainable target. Your immediate success will give you more confidence and that will boost your chances of long-term diet success. You will think of yourself as a winner.

NO

Do you want to lose weight from a particular part of your body?

YES

Try to imagine the shape that you would like to be. Think in positive terms about what you would like to look like, not in negative terms about what you do not like about your current shape. Think of yourself as slender, but shapely. The more realistic you make your image, the more likely you are to be successful.

Do you stop eating when you are no longer hungry?

YES

NO

Learn to use your intuition to help you tell when you are hungry and when you have had enough to eat. Eat when you are hungry and stop when you are not. Concentrate when you are eating.

*A*nxiety

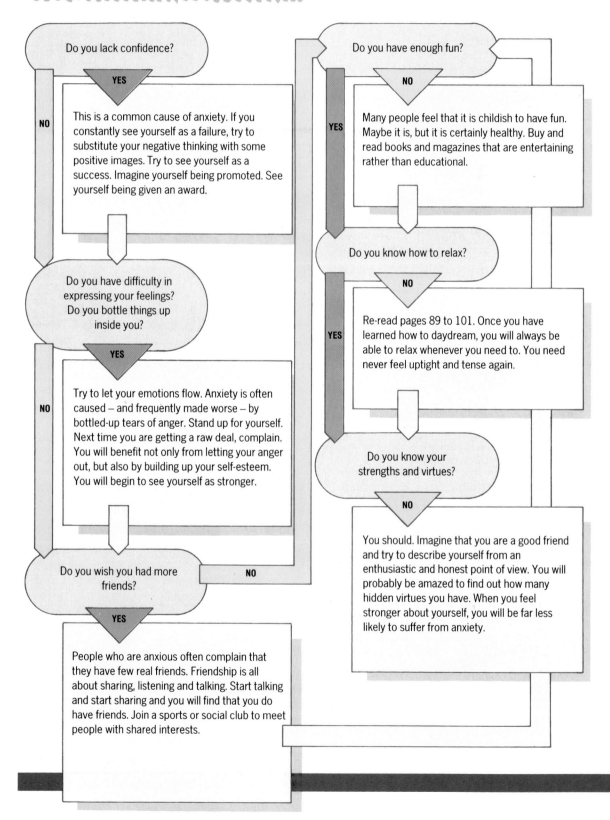

Do you lack confidence?

YES

This is a common cause of anxiety. If you constantly see yourself as a failure, try to substitute your negative thinking with some positive images. Try to see yourself as a success. Imagine yourself being promoted. See yourself being given an award.

NO

Do you have difficulty in expressing your feelings? Do you bottle things up inside you?

YES

Try to let your emotions flow. Anxiety is often caused – and frequently made worse – by bottled-up tears of anger. Stand up for yourself. Next time you are getting a raw deal, complain. You will benefit not only from letting your anger out, but also by building up your self-esteem. You will begin to see yourself as stronger.

NO

Do you wish you had more friends?

NO

YES

People who are anxious often complain that they have few real friends. Friendship is all about sharing, listening and talking. Start talking and start sharing and you will find that you do have friends. Join a sports or social club to meet people with shared interests.

Do you have enough fun?

NO

Many people feel that it is childish to have fun. Maybe it is, but it is certainly healthy. Buy and read books and magazines that are entertaining rather than educational.

YES

Do you know how to relax?

NO

Re-read pages 89 to 101. Once you have learned how to daydream, you will always be able to relax whenever you need to. You need never feel uptight and tense again.

YES

Do you know your strengths and virtues?

NO

You should. Imagine that you are a good friend and try to describe yourself from an enthusiastic and honest point of view. You will probably be amazed to find out how many hidden virtues you have. When you feel stronger about yourself, you will be far less likely to suffer from anxiety.

*H*eadaches

Do you stick up for yourself?

NO →

People who get pushed around or manipulated a lot often suffer from headaches. Learn to assert yourself. (See pages 84 to 85).

YES ↓

Do you ever use your headache as an excuse to avoid doing something?

YES →

We often use headaches as an excuse. The trouble is that, if we use the headache excuse often enough, our bodies will eventually begin to give us headaches on other occasions, too. Our minds learn to use headaches to help us escape from problems. If you use headaches, try to identify the real problems behind the excuse.

NO ↓

Do you know how to relax? Can you daydream?

NO →

You can use a daydream to stop a headache developing or to cure one that has developed. (See pages 92 to 101).

Cancer

Colds

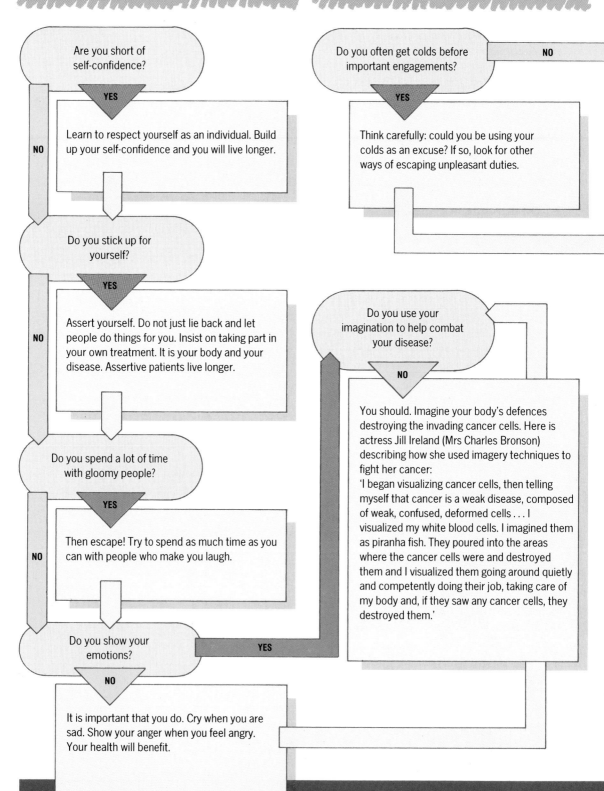

Are you short of self-confidence?

YES → Learn to respect yourself as an individual. Build up your self-confidence and you will live longer.

NO ↓

Do you stick up for yourself?

YES → Assert yourself. Do not just lie back and let people do things for you. Insist on taking part in your own treatment. It is your body and your disease. Assertive patients live longer.

NO ↓

Do you spend a lot of time with gloomy people?

YES → Then escape! Try to spend as much time as you can with people who make you laugh.

NO ↓

Do you show your emotions?

NO → It is important that you do. Cry when you are sad. Show your anger when you feel angry. Your health will benefit.

YES →

Do you often get colds before important engagements?

NO →

YES → Think carefully: could you be using your colds as an excuse? If so, look for other ways of escaping unpleasant duties.

Do you use your imagination to help combat your disease?

NO → You should. Imagine your body's defences destroying the invading cancer cells. Here is actress Jill Ireland (Mrs Charles Bronson) describing how she used imagery techniques to fight her cancer:
'I began visualizing cancer cells, then telling myself that cancer is a weak disease, composed of weak, confused, deformed cells . . . I visualized my white blood cells. I imagined them as piranha fish. They poured into the areas where the cancer cells were and destroyed them and I visualized them going around quietly and competently doing their job, taking care of my body and, if they saw any cancer cells, they destroyed them.'

Do you lack self-confidence?

NO

Do you frequently suffer from boredom?

YES

People who lack self-confidence are especially vulnerable to infection. Improve your self-confidence by thinking of all your virtues. (See pages 68 to 69).

YES

Boredom can increase your chances of getting a cold. Add more purpose and excitement to your life. Give yourself goals and aims and your body will become healthier. If you have a dull job, add thrills to your life by learning a sport or acquiring a hobby at which you can excel.

Arthritis

Do you know how to relax?

NO

It is important that you learn as soon as possible. You can minimize the pains of arthritis by learning how to relax your body properly. (See pages 89 to 101.)

YES

Do you regularly suffer from pain?

YES

Use the techniques described on pages 128 to 129 to help combat pain. Try to see inside each painful joint. See the raw edges of bone grating together uncomfortably and painfully. Now, imagine that you can see a small army of technicians working inside your joints, filling in all the cracks and crevices. Gradually return to this image over the next few days and weeks.

NO

Do you lack self-confidence?   **NO**

YES

This is common among arthritis sufferers. Write out a promotional leaflet for yourself that a Public Relations Agency might prepare. Do not be modest. Think of yourself as the product and then try to sell yourself to the world.

Indigestion

Do you often get angry?

YES

Uncontrolled anger is a common cause of indigestion. Learn how to control your anger. (See page 75.)

NO

Can you relax properly?

NO

Then learn. You will need to practise (see pages 89 to 101) but once you can relax, your stomach will benefit enormously.

Do you have difficulty in moving about?

YES

Every night when you go to bed try to see yourself running. See yourself moving freely and without hindrance. Think of the things you can do – never of the things you cannot do.

Do you have stormy relationships with others?

NO

Do you use your imagination to help control your indigestion?

YES

Take a close look at all your relationships, both private and professional. Use the questions on pages 60 to 61 to help you.

NO

Then try. Imagine that the flow of acid into your stomach is being controlled by a team of special internal plumbers who are hurriedly turning off the taps through which acid pours. At the same time, try to imagine that another team of specialists is busy pouring antacid into your stomach to neutralize the effects of the acid and stop further symptoms.

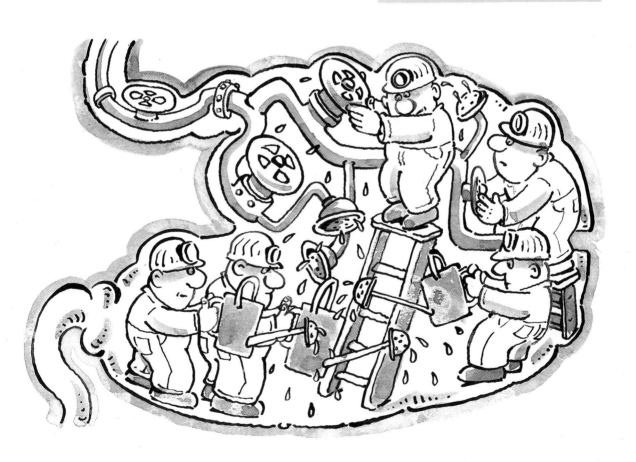

10
How to Help Others

The importance of touch in a loving relationship is nowhere more apparent than in the non-verbal communication between mother and baby.

Watch a mother in the park when her child falls over. He cries. She rushes over and picks him up. The child is soothed almost instantly. His mother's tender touch tells him that he is loved and cared for. You bang your elbow on a sharp table edge. Someone you love is close by. He sees the sudden flash of pain in your eyes, so he rubs your elbow and, as he rubs, so the pain disappears. A woman comes home from work exhausted and tense. She has had a tiring day. Her workload at the office has been horrendous. On the drive home she has been stuck in a five-mile traffic jam. She has a headache and backache. As she sits down, her husband caresses the back of her neck with his fingers, gently massaging away the tension. A boy is out on his first date. He is nervous. He does not know what to expect. His date is nervous, too. It is her first date. They are both too shy to talk, but their bodies talk for them. Through subtle body movements, they communicate with one another. Body language is automatic and transcends all artificial barriers.

Dr Dolores Krieger of New York University has shown that when she uses what she calls 'therapeutic touch', there are measurable improvements in the health of her patients. Dr Robert L. Swearingen, Director of the Colorado Health Institute, has shown that when he touches his patients, they need fewer painkillers and get better much quicker.

Our natural instincts are to get close to one another, to touch one another, when we are in physical or mental pain. Yet for many of us, touch and personal body contact have become too rare an experience.

How often do you touch people you love or care for? Many people feel embarrassed about touching others. They will only hold hands or hug someone if they are sure that no one else is watching. If this sounds like you, try to break down your inhibitions. When you are with someone you love do not be ashamed to hold hands with him or her. When you meet or leave someone you love, give him or her a big hug. It will make both of you feel good. When you meet or say goodbye to a good friend do not be satisfied with a touch of limp fingertips. Shake hands properly, or try a Russian bear hug! In this chapter, I will show you how – and why – we can all help one another with touch and massage and how we can help influence the health of those who are closest to us.

The Importance of Touch

If you have a prejudice against touching people you are close to – particularly in public – try to get rid of it. In the past, it was common for people to think it wrong for courting couples to hold hands, for mothers to breast-feed their babies in public or for couples to exchange kisses. These prejudices were, I suspect, based on nothing more substantial than an unhealthy mixture of religious guilt and unnatural embarrassment.

The truth is, of course, that there is nothing unnatural about sex, courtship and love. Those who disapprove of physical signs of affection are outdated and their prejudices must be discarded. There is nothing intrinsically wrong with two people who love one another cuddling, hugging or kissing in public.

Children, in particular, are susceptible to a lack of affection. Newborn babies should be placed in skin-to-skin contact with their mothers as soon as possible after birth and, for the first few years of life, babies need to be touched frequently by the people who are closest to them. In our society, it is all too easy for a baby to spend the early days in a pram or cot, well away from people. That can be a bad experience. It is well worth remembering that when a child starts to pay an unusual amount of attention to a doll or teddy bear, he or she is crying out for more parental affection and love. There is a real danger that the child who constantly needs to hug his teddy bear is not getting enough love – or enough hugs – from his parents. Do not be shy about touching people – or about allowing people to touch you.

Massage

Massage can help ease tension, soothe tight muscles and relieve pain. Massage helps in a number of quite specific ways. Firstly, it helps to clear away the knots that accumulate in your muscles when you are anxious or nervous. If the tension is not cleared away and the muscles are allowed to stay contracted, waste products, such as lactic acid, collect. These accumulated wastes worsen things by making your muscles stiff and painful and preventing them from relaxing. By massaging these tense areas, it is possible to clear away the accumulated wastes and to relieve muscle stiffness. A good massage can clear knots out of muscles just as easily as wrinkles can be cleared from a sheet by gentle stroking.

Secondly, the personal contact that is an inevitable part of a massage also helps. There is plenty of evidence to show the value of touching. Children who are not cuddled or touched by their parents as they are growing up will develop all sorts of emotional problems. The same thing happens with young animals, too. Gentle massage helps relieve pain and tension by providing sympathy and reassurance.

Thirdly, there are some experts who believe that massage does not just relax the muscles but also soothes the mind. Wilhelm Reich, a psychologist who practised at the turn of the century, believed that some people hide their emotions in their muscles. It is certainly true that many people also feel mentally relaxed after a massage.

Finally, massage has very specific and positive pain-relieving effects. It helps to stimulate the production of endorphins, the body's internally produced pain-relieving hormones. Also, it stimulates the production of sensory impulses; these are carried along the body's larger nerve fibres, and block the transmission of pain messages through into the spinal cord.

If you want to try to help a friend or loved one by giving him/her a massage you can do so quite easily. You do not need a lot of training; nor do you need any special equipment. The following are important tips to help you give a massage safely and correctly.

Remember that massage should never be painful. If you are giving a massage, tell your patient to let you know if anything hurts. If you are receiving a massage, make sure you tell your masseur if anything hurts you.

Before you start, both of you should be comfortable. Clothes should be loose and light, the room should be pleasantly warm and the lighting should be dim. You may find some soothing, background music helpful. The best place in most homes to perform a massage is on the floor. A foam mat or a couple of rugs spread out on the carpet will provide adequate comfort. If the subject is going to have the front of his/her body massaged, put one small cushion under his/her head and another under his/her knees. You should not need cushions to massage the patient's back.

Oil lubricates the skin and makes it easier to give a massage. If you do not like oil, you can use talcum powder, which works almost as well.

Do not worry if you have never given a massage before, simply follow your intuition. Start with a general massage involving all areas of the body, and concentrate your efforts on places that are sore or tense. Be cautious when moving joints and avoid the spine completely.

There are many different types of massage movement. Start by using the flat of your hand to stroke the muscles. Try rubbing the skin and experiment with a little gentle slapping and tapping of the skin to stimulate it.

Finally, do not despair if you want a massage but there is no one to give you one. You *can* give yourself a half massage. You will not be able to reach the whole of your body (unless you are a contortionist) but you will be able to reach many of the parts which normally ache. For example, if you have a headache or a sore neck, you can help yourself by kneading your shoulders and the back of your neck with your fingers. You may be able to get rid of a headache by massaging the area just between your eyes, the areas to the side of your eyes and the areas just in front of your ears. You can massage your hands and feet quite easily by working your way over them, starting from the tips of your fingers and toes and moving towards the palm of your hand and the ball of your foot.

It is sometimes possible to soothe a troubled person simply by massaging his/her skin with one finger. When I was a junior hospital doctor, I used this technique with some success when nursing patients of all ages. It seemed to work particularly well with confused, elderly patients and with very small babies who were crying and keeping everyone else awake. I suspect that this type of massage worked best with those at opposite ends of the age spectrum simply because they were least likely to feel embarrassed or shocked.

The Healing Touch

There is now considerable evidence to show that the 'laying on of hands' can have a healing effect. One of the first experiments was performed by Bernard Grad, a biochemist working at McGill University in Montreal. He anaesthetized some mice, made small cuts in their skin and divided them into two groups. The mice in the first group were left to heal naturally, without any treatment. The mice in the second group were healed by a professional healer and they got better quicker than the first group of mice.

Even more convincing has been the relatively recent work of Dolores Krieger, now a doctor but at the time a Professor of Nursing at New York University and one of the best-known healers in the world. Krieger convinced many sceptical doctors of the power of healing by touch by running controlled clinical trials in which blood changes produced by healing were measured in a laboratory. You really cannot get better evidence than that.

One of the most remarkable modern discoveries is that, although there may be some benefits to be gained by visiting a professional healer, most patients can use healing techniques themselves. Anyone, it seems, can become a healer. You can use your hidden healing powers on your friends, your relatives or even on yourself!

All you have to do to use your body's own healing powers is to place your hands on or close to your patient's body. You then merely project a feeling of well-being, comfort and good health from your body to theirs. Try to feel the strength radiating from your hands on to the troubled area.

There is a simple experiment that you can try if you want to check your own healing potential. Start by putting your hands close together, with your fingers pointing away from you, as though you were praying. Do not let your hands touch but get them as close together as you possibly can. Next, separate your hands by two inches or so and keep them apart for a few seconds. Then return them to the original position – close together without actually touching. Keep your hands in that position for a few more seconds and then separate them by four inches. Once again keep them apart for a few seconds. After returning your hands to the original position, separate them by six inches. Do this as slowly as you possibly can and remember to hold each position for a few seconds at a time. Finally, separate your hands by eight or ten inches and then gradually bring them back together again in rather jerky, two-inch movements.

You will quite probably feel a strange sort of bounciness as you do so, as though the air were being compressed between your hands, and you will probably also notice a change in the skin temperature of your hands. They may become a little warmer, they may tingle or they may feel noticeably cooler. The change, which is otherwise inexplicable, is a sign that you have the healing touch!

The Healing Smile

Norman Cousins said that he moved out of hospital and into a hotel because a hospital is no place for a sick person. I think he was probably right. To refresh my memory, I wandered into a large, general hospital the other day and was reminded just how depressing these places can be.

The building itself was cold and cheerless and inside no one seemed to have made any effort at all to make the place hospitable. (It is funny that hospitable is the one word that you would rarely use to describe hospitals.) The walls were painted a remarkably nauseating mixture of brown, green and cream. The only relief was provided by some of the worst and most depressing, dark pictures I have seen since the last time I was in a hospital. Most of them were portraits of elderly men with mutton-chop whiskers and snooty stares, remembered now largely for their vanity. Other corridors were studded with terrible attempts at modern art – all, presumably, donated by benefactors who had enough good sense not to hang them in their own homes!

Everywhere I looked there were forbidding notices. 'Do not do this.' 'Do not do that.' 'Do not even dream of doing the other.' Each notice seemed designed to give any visitor the impression that if he so much as dared even to think of stepping out of line, in no time at all he would be on a cold, marble slab with a surgeon hovering over him ready to exact the price for disobedience.

There were flashing lights and buzzers, and an apparently endless stream of self-important administrators hurrying along the corridors with briefcases and folders full of papers. The atmosphere reeked of that special hospital blend of antiseptic, starch and disinfectant that they must mix up and spray around the wards at least three times a day. The floors were cold, hard and terribly noisy. The high ceilings allowed the noise from the clattering trolleys to bounce around in an endless, headache-provoking circle of sound. If someone had tried to design a hospital that patients and visitors would have found uncomfortable and unfriendly, they could not have done it more effectively.

It was visiting time while I was there – a truly depressing experience. While they waited to be herded into the wards, the visitors were left huddled together in the corridors. Their shoulders were hunched, their faces were grim, grey and pinched and they looked terrified. The few who had managed to crowd into the small tea room were drinking an awful brown brew from cracked, thick, green cups.

When the doors to the wards were finally opened, the visitors trudged through and gathered around the beds of their loved ones like ghosts at a funeral feast. The conversations were quiet, with lots of whispering, muttering and shaking of heads. There was not a smile to be seen or a laugh to be heard.

At the end of the allotted time, the visitors stood up as one, put their chairs away, straightened the bedclothes, offered sterile, cautious kisses and tiptoed away. They paused only to offer brief, final waves from the ward entrance, before hurrying out into the comfort of the cold and the dark and the rain. Abandoned by their visitors, the patients were left staring at their brown paper bags full of grapes, their crumpled copies of the local newspaper ('HORRIFIC ROAD CRASH KILLS SEVEN' screamed the almost inevitable headlines) and their bottles of orange squash.

What makes all this absolutely unforgivable is that we now know for sure that if you keep hospital patients as happy, comfortable and

Genuine affection and laughter – two vital ingredients of a healthy relationship.

contented as possible, they will suffer far less pain and will get better quicker. If you make patients smile, they will suffer far fewer complications. If you provide them with comfortable, cheerful surroundings, they will be ready to go home sooner.

This knowledge is not new, of course. Several thousand years ago in India and Greece they knew all about it. They knew that it was important to keep hospitals as cheery as possible if you wanted your patients to get better. They played soft music, and sweet-smelling flowers were everywhere. They planned their colour schemes carefully and prepared food to tempt and stimulate jaded appetites. They did all this not just because it was kind, but because it was sensible. It made simple, sound clinical sense!

Today we have lost our way. Although there are excellent exceptions, too many of our hospitals are badly designed, badly organized and badly run. They are, too often, run for the benefit of those who work in and administer them rather than for the benefit of the patients. We should paint the walls in *all* our hospitals in bright, cheerful colours. There should be beautiful pictures, prints or photographs in them. There should be video recorders on all the wards and supplies of good, amusing movies should be circulated. There should be music cassettes and magazines freely available and a good library of amusing paperbacks. Clowns should visit the wards regularly and hairdressers and beauticians should be provided for the patients. All the dull, depressing, forbidding notices should be torn down and there should be far fewer rules and regulations. Nurses and doctors should be encouraged to dress in bright clothes and everything possible should be done to make patients feel less threatened and less vulnerable.

All this will take time. Meanwhile, if you are planning to visit anyone in hospital (or in a nursing home, convalescent home or sick room), there is quite a lot that you can do yourself. Turn up with a smile and a few interesting stories, wear something colourful and carry imaginative gifts. Take holiday brochures rather than the sad news of Mrs Hampton's budgie's death. Remember that smiles, like scowls and yawns, are infectious. When you smile, the person you are visiting will smile – and when we smile, we feel better.

ndex

Page numbers shown in *italic* type
indicate illustrations